RECREATING THE PERIOD GARDEN

General Editor:

GRAHAM STUART THOMAS

OBE, VMH, DHM, VMM

Gardens Consultant to the National Trust

COLLINS

8 Grafton Street · London W1

1984

First published in
Great Britain 1984 by

William Collins Sons & Co Ltd
London · Glasgow · Sydney ·
Auckland · Toronto ·
Johannesburg

The National Trust
36 Queen Anne's Gate
London SW1

© Swallow Publishing Ltd 1984

Conceived and produced by
Swallow Publishing Limited
32 Hermes Street
London N1

Editor Sarah Snape
Copy editor Mary Trewby
Designer Malcolm Smythe
Design assistants Sue Brinkhurst
and Laurence Grinter
Picture researchers Melissa Hay
and Liz Eddison
Practical features Melissa Hay,
A. Barry (92-3), K. Sanecki (50, 52)

Recreating the period garden.
1. Landscape gardening
I. Thomas, Graham Stuart
712'.6   SB472

ISBN 0 00 216485 X

All statements in this book giving
information and advice are believed to be
true and accurate at the time of going to
press, but neither the authors nor the
publishers can accept legal liability for
errors or omissions.

Set in Palatino by Dorchester Typesetting
Group
Printed in Italy by S.A.G.D.O.S., Milan

ACKNOWLEDGEMENTS
*Swallow Books gratefully
acknowledge the assistance given to
them in the production of this book
by the following people and
organizations. We apologise to
anyone we may have unwittingly
omitted to mention.*

Illustrators
Rhoda Burns 90/91, 176/7; Bernard
Fallon 51, 92/3; Andrew Farmer
131, 152/3; Elsa Godfrey 48/9, 108/
9, 111, 127, 159, 160/1, 168, 169;
Laurence Grinter 31, 106, 144;
Malcolm Smythe 56; David Tetley
32, 33, 141.

Photographic credits
The Architect and Building News,
43 (t&b); John Bly, 165 (m);
Cambridge University Collection,
29; Country Life Magazine, 90;
Crowther of Syon Lodge, 155, 158

(b); Sue Deacon, 106, 185, 187, 188;
Paul Edwards, 128, 129, 132, 148
(r), 149 (r), 159, 162 (t&bl), 163 (r),
165 (t), 166 (l), 167 (l&r), 171 (t),
182; Melissa Hay, 52, 53 (l), 58, 59,
75 (b), 110 (both), 124 (l), 126, 127,
138 (t), 148 (l), 186 (t); The Iris
Hardwick Library of Photographs,
46, 47, 48, 49, 50 (bl), 53 (t), 69, 87,
88, 96, 99, 103, 107, 109, 112, 113,
136, 140, 141, 142, 145 (tr), 146
(l&r), 149 (l), 150 (both), 151, 154 (t),
156 (l&r), 166 (r), 168 (l), 172, 174
(b), 178, 180, 183 (l), 186 (b), 188 (t),
191 (b); Anthony Lord, 39;
L F Knight Limited, 183 (r); Paul
Miles, 40, 83 (all), 85, 86, 89, 134,
138 (b), 145 (tl), 169 (r), 176, 191 (t);
The National Trust, 75 (t), 124 (t l),
135 (l), 174 (t), 179, 190 (b); Lady
O'Neill, 57, 62, 63, 71, 78, 79;
Anthony du Gard Pasley, 36, 37
(all), 125 (both), 137, 145 (b), 154 (b),
190 (t); W. Richardson & Co Ltd

173; The Royal Horticultural
Society, 10, 12 (l&r), 13, 14, 15
(t&b), 16, 17, 18, 19, (l&r), 20, 21,
23, 25 (t&b), 26, 60, 64, 67 (t),
68, 95, 98, 100, 101; Graham
Stuart Thomas 42, 44, 50 (br), 67
(b), 74 (both), 84, 94, 122, 135 (r),
139, 153, 162 (br), 163 (bl), 171 (b);
Reginald Thompson, 164, (m&b);
Victoria & Albert Museum, 114;
Fred Whitsey, 41, 116 (t&b), 117
(all), 119, 120, 121 (t&b), 189.

The illustration on page 164 (t)
is from J B Papworth's *Rural
Residences* (1818); and on page 165
(b), from William Robinson's *The
Parks, Promenades and Gardens of
Paris* (1869).

Key to abbreviations
(t) top (b) bottom (l) left
(r) right (m) middle

Captions to cover photographs

The Old Rose walk at Hidcote Manor
Garden, Gloucestershire. *(front).*

Espalier fruit trees and forcing pots
in an old walled kitchen garden.

Trellis-work pillars make a rose
pergola at Bodnant, North Wales.

Brilliant colour contrast in the Red
Border at Hidcote.

Pot grown *Agave* by the lily pond at
Hidcote.

Pansies in a stone urn at Ascott
House, Buckinghamshire.

The Yew Hedge Garden at
Knightshayes Court, Devon.

CONTENTS

*Special features contributed by *Melissa Hay, †A. Barry*

FOREWORD

Graham Stuart Thomas

Many of us start gardening in a small area of ground in our parents' garden. After this early start, apart from a certain amount of grass-cutting, hedge-clipping and the like, the pursuit of gardening remains in abeyance until we own a house with its surrounding plot of land. Then gardening starts in earnest if we are that way inclined. The area may be already laid out, or it may be a virgin plot. The desire comes to make or adjust it to our needs or preferences – certain areas may be needed for vegetables, a swimming pool, a boxed area of sand for the children; the planting of a favourite fruit tree or discarded Christmas tree; homes have to be found for gifts of plants, or for purchases made at bazaars or garden centres. Roses are usually considered, also the conveniences connected with the working of the garden – paths, compost heap, lawn, and a paved area for sitting; seats, vases for plants and the general decoration of our new garden. It can so easily become a collection of what may appear to be essentials, but unrelated and disconnected. Tempted by colourful catalogues, there is also often the urge to go one better than our neighbours, coupled with the avid desire for beauty to contrast what may be our drab working lives. At times the infinity of alternatives can be bewildering.

Without claiming to be a book on down-to-earth garden design, of which there are many available, this volume seeks to answer the many questions that crop up – the why, the when and the how. It puts before you the underlying reasons which can make one garden different from another, and shows how by learning from the past we can give every garden a new twist, style and perspective without transgressing the traditional in every kind of art connected with gardening. In the following pages an assembly of garden experts puts before you well reasoned chapters on all the fundamentals which govern the design of gardens.

It is, I think, a particularly opportune book. With our leisure time increasing yearly one of the great pursuits is the visiting of houses and gardens open to the public, both great and small. In these are to be found a limitless number of ideas for every feature and style, old and new. Fostered by the many books on the history of garden design, and the activities of the Garden History Society and the National Council for the Conservation of Plants and Gardens, our ideas on garden design can easily become confused, so vast is the canvas spread before us. We are apt to consider the historical designs of great gardens only, not grasping the fact that it is within the compass of us all, in both large and small plots, to capture a facet of history in design, embellishment and planting.

We are apt to visit gardens open to the public and gasp at the beauty spread before us. That is, of course, what the owners of such gardens hope we shall do. But many great gardens have been designed piecemeal and embellished by succeeding generations. In addition, very few gardens ever remain exactly as they were intended; they are always changing owing to the forces of nature, and this we cannot alter. It is moreover what makes gardening different from all other arts.

Turning now from the sublime to the ridiculous, instead of time-honoured lawns and age-old trees, ancient shrubberies and borders, marble statues and leaden urns and vases, we sometimes are confronted with something quite different. Smaller gardens of today may have a number of disparate features: a historic marble or stone ornament may be the prized piece, but accompanying it may be a Victorian seat or cast iron vase, a plastic pool, modern wooden trellis, concrete paving mixed with old hand-made bricks and plants and flowers from all over the world – as like as not 'improved' by hybridizing since their introduction to this country which has been due to exploring the world over the centuries. There might even be the gnome or miniature windmill, and all this might be grouped round a house built at any time from medieval days until the 1980s. To some all this might not be distressing or even disturbing, but we are all consciously or unconsciously educated by what we see in other gardens or in books. Gradually the suitability of one thing to another becomes borne into our minds and this is where enquiry starts. It is at this moment in our awareness that this book will most opportunely help. By observing, sifting and discarding ideas through deep thought and study, every garden can be transformed and made different in character from all others and yet be an authentic representation of an historic style. Ornamental horticulture has veered in many ways during its long transition from the days of the first Elizabeth.

But this is only half of gardening as we know it. Chapter 1 sets forth all of it as an art, but the craft remains. The craft of gardening made itself a niche long before the art reached such eminence. Plants were originally grown in prepared plots for their value to life itself. Not all of us want a garden to be solely concerned with art for our recreation and subtle enjoyment.

We may also enjoy the satisfaction that comes from raising successive crops of fruits and vegetables such as has been practised over the centuries in cottage gardens as well as in the vast walled gardens of the great mansions. In terms of mere size the latter are things of the past, but the skills remain the same for smaller gardens. There is much satisfaction in contemplating, let alone profiting from, the fancy training of fruit trees and the interplay of beans and cabbages, onions and carrots, their impeccable rows giving delight.

There are, too, the herbs, both medicinal and culinary, which strangely unite both the art and the craft of gardening. For a hundred years or more herbs have been grown in patterned plots reminiscent of ornamental gardens in more distant times.

But perhaps we are not wanting our garden to need a lot of work to keep it reasonably trim. The severe patterns of knot gardens and the intriguing scrolls of more elaborate parterres can be recreated today; they require a minimum of work thanks to mechanical aids and the occasional use of weedkillers and other short cuts to the expenditure of labour.

It is through the study of the history of garden art and craft that we can arrive at a satisfying perspective of this, our oldest pursuit and hobby, and I am confident that this book will awaken latent interest among all kinds of gardeners. Our time can be devoted to study with increasing enjoyment. This book goes hand in hand with *Putting Back the Style*, originally published in hardback by Evans Brothers Ltd in 1982, which had so good a reception. With the two at hand everyone will benefit by a new awareness of style in both home and garden.

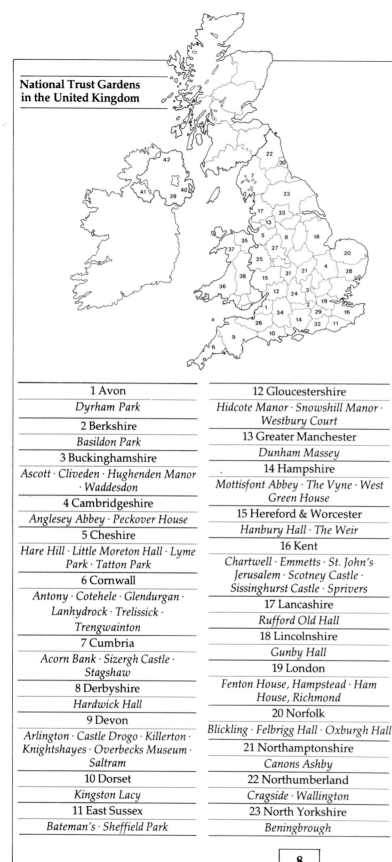

National Trust Gardens in the United Kingdom

24 Oxfordshire

Buscot · Greys Court

25 Shropshire

Benthall Hall · Dudmaston

26 Somerset

Barrington Court · Cleveden Court · Dunster Castle · Lytes Cary · Montacute · Tintinhull House

27 Staffordshire

Moseley Old Hall · Shugborough · Wightwick

28 Suffolk

Ickworth · Melford Hall

29 Surrey

Claremont · Polesden Lacey · Winkworth Arboretum

30 Tyne & Wear

Washington Old Hall

31 Warwickshire

Baddesley Clinton · Charlecote Park · Farnborough Hall · Packwood House · Upton House

32 West Sussex

Nymans · Petworth Park · Standen · Uppark · Wakehurst Place

33 West Yorkshire

East Riddlesden Hall

34 Wiltshire

The Courts, Holt · Stourhead

Wales

35 Clwyd

Chirk Castle · Erddig

36 Dyfed

Colby Lodge

37 Gwynedd

Bodnant · Penrhyn · Plas Newydd · Plas-yn-Rhiw

38 Powys

Powis Castle

Northern Ireland

39 Co. Armagh

Ardress · The Argory

40 Co. Down

Castle Ward · Mount Stewart · Rowallane

41 Co. Fermanagh

Florence Court ʻ

42 Co. Londonderry

Springhill

1 Avon

Dyrham Park

2 Berkshire

Basildon Park

3 Buckinghamshire

Ascott · Cliveden · Hughenden Manor · Waddesdon

4 Cambridgeshire

Anglesey Abbey · Peckover House

5 Cheshire

Hare Hill · Little Moreton Hall · Lyme Park · Tatton Park

6 Cornwall

Antony · Cotehele · Glendurgan · Lanhydrock · Trelissick · Trengwainton

7 Cumbria

Acorn Bank · Sizergh Castle · Stagshaw

8 Derbyshire

Hardwick Hall

9 Devon

Arlington · Castle Drogo · Killerton · Knightshayes · Overbecks Museum · Saltram

10 Dorset

Kingston Lacy

11 East Sussex

Bateman's · Sheffield Park

12 Gloucestershire

Hidcote Manor · Snowshill Manor · Westbury Court

13 Greater Manchester

Dunham Massey

14 Hampshire

Mottisfont Abbey · The Vyne · West Green House

15 Hereford & Worcester

Hanbury Hall · The Weir

16 Kent

Chartwell · Emmetts · St. John's Jerusalem · Scotney Castle · Sissinghurst Castle · Sprivers

17 Lancashire

Rufford Old Hall

18 Lincolnshire

Gunby Hall

19 London

Fenton House, Hampstead · Ham House, Richmond

20 Norfolk

Blickling · Felbrigg Hall · Oxburgh Hall

21 Northamptonshire

Canons Ashby

22 Northumberland

Cragside · Wallington

23 North Yorkshire

Beningbrough

1
THE GARDEN IN HISTORY

I t is difficult to determine when the ornamental garden as we know it re-emerged in Europe after the long disruption following the collapse of the Roman empire. Many monasteries, palaces, and castles had gardens during the Middle Ages, but while existing contemporary descriptions emphasize their delightful qualities, it seems certain that these were incidental to more utilitarian interests.

Similarities can be seen in the emergence of gardening anywhere. When an area was subject to repeated invasion, civil strife or attacks of banditry, walled enclosures were used for defence; a reliable degree of peace was needed before gardens could spread outside the town or castle walls. And while a thriving town or city could extend farms and market gardens through the surrounding countryside, any isolated establishment, whether a monastery, a country house, or a simple cottage, had, until quite recently, to be self-sufficient; the first use of a garden, therefore, was to grow crops for food and supply plants for medicinal use.

Medieval gardening was dominated by this approach to planting, and was generally restricted to walled areas and courtyards, the most common shape being a square subdivided into further squares. Within this limiting framework some recreational elements were introduced: features such as seats and turf banks, arbours and trellised walks for shade, and in Mediterranean countries, especially those where Arabic influence prevailed, fountains, cascades and water channels to counteract the often excessive heat.

Contact with the Arab world, established by the Crusades, led to a first great wave of plants being introduced into western Europe, and the redevelopment of some ingenious horticultural techniques, particularly grafting. The greenhouse is said to have been invented by Albertus Magnus in the early thirteenth century, and mazes and the planting of flower-beds by season may have appeared by the fourteenth.

Combining the ornamental and practical: the fishponds at the Villa d'Este, Tivoli, in the seventeenth century.

Rediscovering the Classical Garden

The fourteenth century saw an increasing interest, on the part of Italian scholars, in the antiquities of their ancient Roman ancestors; by the early part of the following century, leading architects were making a radical break with the recent past, and returning to the forms of Roman building, which they regarded as the true style from which the world had deviated. While merchants and nobility began to build villas in the classical manner, the works of Pliny the younger and his contemporaries were eagerly scanned for descriptions of the ancient Roman style of gardening. Leon Battista Alberti, in the first architectural work to be circulated as a printed book (published in the mid-1480s), outlined the essential features of every property: the villa should be set on a hill, for views of city and countryside; it should have open galleries and a vine-covered pergola for shade and sunlight, and be cooled by flowing water and fountains; it should boast a grotto and a kitchen garden of fruit trees; the open portion should have box-edged paths, cypresses planted in rows, topiary (shaping the letters to the owner's name, for example), stone vases of flowers, and statuary. The garden should be laid out in the geometrical patterns most approved in building – rectangles, circles, semi-circles, and the like.

The gardens that were created in this first flush of enthusiasm for the antique have now disappeared, and it is difficult to recapture their atmosphere. To a great extent, despite Alberti's talk of open galleries, they continued the medieval tradition of enclosed gardens; radical breaks with the past are more easily recommended than achieved. Indeed, it is difficult to tell to what extent some of the most striking devices of the period drew solely on Roman texts, and to what extent on the traditions which evolved in the interim. Alberti implies that he had seen grottoes with walls naturalistically smeared with green wax to suggest slime (which hardly seems a Roman practice); and the explosive spread of complicated topiary patterns hints at an already well-developed programme of training in a complicated art. The Villa Rucellai, on which Alberti may have advised, contained trees shaped as 'spheres, porticoes, temples, vases … giants, men, women, warriors, a harpy, philosophers, Popes, Cardinals' – even more complex tableaux were executed elsewhere.

By the end of the fifteenth century, works of sculpture – antique or modern – were beginning to replace topiary as decorations. Slower to develop was Alberti's notion of the garden as a viewpoint for the surrounding country. During his lifetime, imaginative designers such as Michelozzo began to lay out gardens that employed more than one level; but, as in the Villa Medici at Fiesole, begun in 1458, the connecting stairs were hidden – they ran from the garden through underground rooms. The ancient Romans had no advice to give on terracing the grounds of a villa, and similarly most early Renaissance gardens remained flat. Each level or major subdivision of the garden was laid out as a unit by itself, separate from the others, with its own axis of symmetry; each section would comprise compartments of box, grass, or flowers arranged in geometrical figures, each different from its neighbour.

In 1495, Charles VIII of France invaded Italy and sent back accounts of the wonders he saw in the gardens he visited. On his return, he brought back a small colony of Italian artists to beautify the dwellings of his court. So the ideas of the new gardening spread beyond the Alps, and were accommodated within the medieval conventions of gardening in northern Europe. Early in the sixteenth century, Louis XII's new garden at Blois boasted a series of terraces extending from the château, each with its independent axis and geometrical compartments; by 1520 similar compartments, called knots in England, were being created at Hampton Court.

Mastery over Nature

While the gardeners of the North were still setting out their patterns within square enclosures, and struggling to translate Italian concepts such as the pergola into appropriate equivalents, perhaps galleries of trellis-work, gardens in Italy itself were being opened out and transformed, using the rediscovered rules of perspective. The pioneering work, executed at the beginning of the sixteenth century, was the courtyard of the Belvedere, adjoining the Vatican Palace, where Bramante had connected the three descending levels of the enclosed space by a series of prominent staircases and ramps. The next generation began to put Bramante's devices to work on the less enclosed hillside villas. Now, stairs, loggias, walks and cascades were combined to form an axis extending from the house and linking all the hitherto independent levels, and it was possible to move from one level to another without losing sight of the composition.

Several ambitious projects were under way by the 1550s, refashioning entire

A garden design by Vredeman de Vries, 1583, showing the use of trellised walkways and intricate patterning.

Sixteenth-century landscaping on a hillside site: a view in the Boboli Gardens, Florence.

hillsides. At the Boboli Gardens in Florence, the ground was shaped into a horseshoe amphitheatre; at the Villa d'Este at Tivoli, a network of crossing axes, one lined by a hundred fountains (the water 'organ'), led up a gentle slope to the hilltop with its spectacular views. There, whereas the house was sited to enjoy far-reaching views, the garden itself was still self-contained, although it was increasingly defined by contrast with the surrounding landscape. At the Villa Farnese at Caprarola, Vignola cut two symmetrical gardens into the hillside above the house at an angle to each other, filling the triangle between them with a plantation of trees to suggest a wilderness. Small areas of irregular planting were gradually being incorporated into the garden proper for contrast with the more obviously planned features; this practice found its English analogy in Francis Bacon's plan for a heath of 'natural wildness' in his ideal garden.

In the flatter gardens of France, England and the Netherlands, instead of such large-scale terracing, mounds were created artificially; they provided a prospect over the garden itself and the surrounding fields. In smaller gardens an elevated pavilion sufficed. And cascades were replaced by canals, often direct survivals of defensive moats, which framed or flanked the garden.

Features, such as grottoes and sculptures, that had previously been included simply because the ancient Romans had used them, were acquiring additional meaning as elements of a symbolic whole: gardens were being organized as planned sequences of walks and views designed as illustration. Today, their meanings are often obscure; the garden at the Villa Orsini at Bomarzo, for example, has provoked many conflicting interpretations. The more easily grasped are those celebrating the resident family with sculpture groups, which invoke their mythical ancestors or pun on their name (as with the sculpted bears, *ursi*, at the Villa Orsini), or which glorified Italy or Rome (the Villa d'Este included a scale model of the contemporary idea of antique Rome). In general, a broad recurring pattern can be detected, contrasting civilization, represented by architectural works,

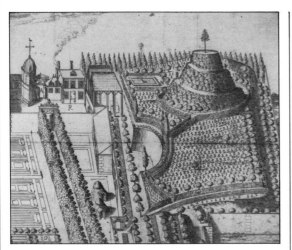

The mount in the 'jardin royal' in Paris in the 1630s gives vertical scale to a largely flat site.

geometrical layouts and topiary, with unredeemed nature, represented by sections of informal planting and naturalistic grottoes. The grottoes of the later sixteenth century could be exceedingly ornate, as in French examples by Palissy, crawling with realistically carved and coloured animal forms, and, inside, displaying the forms of classical architecture, but encrusted with exaggerated stonework. In such a grotto the normal expectations of life could be turned upside down; the visitor might be assaulted by concealed jets of water, for instance; at one point the skylight in the Boboli grotto was designed as a fishtank, so that the visitor would be disconcerted by seeing water overhead (a device copied throughout Europe).

These trick water-jets had begun to appear about 1500, and by the end of the century were not confined to grottoes, but emerged anywhere – from the pavement, from seats, from statues. Fountains with sculptural groups depicting mythical or rustic scenes were considered an important art form, but even more admired than these were mechanical devices that actually enacted scenes or played music. There had been a continuous tradition of automata at the Byzantine court – the techniques were brought to Italy by refugees from the Turkish conquest of Constantinople in 1453 – but the Italians preferred to think of them as a revival of the inventions of Hero of Alexandria. The human ability to rival nature was best shown in the creation of gardens such as Pratolino, whose grotto contained a mechanical Pan playing his pipes, a triton blowing a conch, and a nymph emerging from a rock astride a shell. For Heidelberg, in the 1610s, Salomon de Caus devised a singing fountain and a statue of Hercules that emitted a musical tone when touched by sunlight. A Renaissance garden must have been full of sound; the water organ at the Villa d'Este seems a comparatively crude example.

The conquest of nature could be represented in myriad ways, from a fountain cast in the shape of a tree to a real tree subdued into supporting an elaborate treehouse, as at Pratolino. But a fartherreaching demonstration of this mastery was provided by the cultivation of exotic flowers. Ambassadors to the Turkish court, struck by the unfamiliar plants they saw, introduced such novelties as tulips, hyacinths and fritillaries into Europe. The collecting mania roused by the tulip is well known, but the collection of exotics, and their use in the garden, fast became a general passion. The idea arose of uniting the plants of disparate parts of the world to recreate a primeval paradise. (It was not lost on the learned of the day that the word paradise signified a park.)

The first botanic gardens were set up in Pisa and Padua in 1543-5; Paris may have had such a garden in the 1570s, although the Jardin du Roi was not established until 1626; Leiden followed suit in 1587, Montpellier in 1593, Oxford in 1621. In the Protestant countries of the North, in particular, where successful experiments were being made in cultivation under glass, some radicals speculated that the effects of Adam's fall might be overcome and the differences of the seasons annulled through scientific gardening, and year-round prosperous cultivation achieved. Such was the effect of the English climate, however, that knots still had to be made with coloured earths or stones if a pattern was wanted that would remain beautiful in winter.

Ideas of Order

In 1598, the Villa Aldobrandini was begun at Frascati. Here, for the first time, the central axis was made the dominating feature of the garden, and the house was sited so that it overlooked the one essential view – a characteristic of many seventeenth-century Italian gardens. Simultaneously, the French were designing symmetrical layouts, with matching patterned compartments on either side of the main axis. Claude Mollet, head gardener to Henri IV, argued that the garden ought to be treated as one great compartment. The result was an increase in the level ground immediately in front of the house devoted to ornamental patterning (the area now named the parterre). The panels of ground within the parterre, often no longer square but extending as part of a vista from the house, could comprise designs that were asymmetrical in themselves, but, when seen from the windows in combination with the other panels, revealed one overall symmetrical pattern.

From the copious variety of the Renaissance garden, Mollet and his contemporaries selected a few essentials – the parterre, lawns, water, and framing

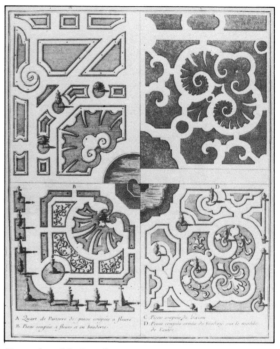

Examples of designs for parterre panels – individually asymmetrical, but part of an overall pattern.

bosquets (parcels of woodland) – from which to assemble gardens on the new principle of one central framework. The climax of this development was reached in the work of André Le Nôtre at Vaux-le-Vicomte near Versailles, and a series of associated gardens, including that at Louis XIV's Palace of Versailles. The dazzling reputation of Le Nôtre's works, and the recording of his principles in a manual (*La Théorie et la Pratique du Jardinage* by Dezallier d'Argenville) published in 1709, ensured that his style, with local modifications, spread throughout Europe. It remained the favoured model until the middle of the eighteenth century. Versailles, which was altered continually over a period of fifty years, became the single most influential garden in history.

For the framework of a Le Nôtre garden, the central axis – the view from the house –

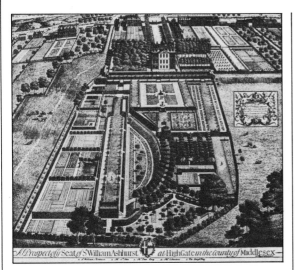

The French formal style adapted to a small English site: Ashurst Manor in London, in the early eighteenth century. It later became the site of Highgate Cemetery.

The frontispiece to 'De Nieuwe . . . Neederlandse Hovenier', 1716, showing a Dutch parterre – a style adapted to restricted sites.

was extended to dominate the countryside: the main vista at Versailles stretches for over 2 km (1¼ miles). Ideally, this linking of the garden with the horizon suggests order reaching to infinity. At Versailles this notion was exploited politically in the choice of statuary: Louis XIV, the Sun King, from whom power radiated through the kingdom as the avenues radiated through his grounds, was invoked by sculptures and fountains representing episodes in the myths of the sun god Apollo. This sort of political symbolism and demonstration of intended omnipotence was neither possible nor desirable for all of Le Nôtre's imitators; in England, in particular, gardens in this style were often laid out to one side of the house, thus deflecting the perceived lines of power.

Seventeenth-century treatises recommended that a harmony be established between garden and landscape, that art be used only to set off the beauties of nature. Nature and art are, of course, rather flexible terms, but this impression of balance was important to Le Nôtre. The immediate impression, apart from the axial vista, was made by the parterre. Beyond this, a complex foreground yielded to simpler features as the vista lengthened, and bosquets screened the views to the sides of the main axis. From this axis, further canals or rides (a garden the size of Versailles was meant to be traversed by horse) extended symmetrically, leading to views or enclosures; sculptures, fountains, or garden buildings served as eye-catchers at the ends of such views. A favourite device was the *patte-d'oie*, or goosefoot, a set of three radiating avenues, the ends of which could be held in a single view; in later Dutch gardens this became a major organizing principle, replacing the single axis. Some vistas served as prospects over woods or

Fanciful rockwork at Versailles provides a setting for sculptures depicting scenes from La Fontaine's Fables.

those of (apparent) nature now gave way to one unifying system of order. Grottoes and fountains with naturalistic rockwork were subordinated to their architectural settings, and no longer were insects and lizards depicted crawling over grotto stonework. The more emphatic attempts to rival nature, by elaborate topiary and automata, also fell from favour. Where visitors were deceived, it was not by trick water-jets but by carefully contrived illusions of perspective. Some enclosures were laid out in an irregular manner, with winding paths among trees or serpentine streams criss-crossing the ground; at the turn of the century, Dufresny laid out an informal garden at Versailles that was said to have inspired William Kent in England, while the designs of Batty Langley in the 1720s (also in England) simply multiplied the number of such compartments. But irregular terrain was best matched by an accompanying architectural work, as at Vaux-le-Vicomte where it framed a model of the Egyptian pyramids. And if a fountain depicting a scene was impressive, even more so was a fountain that relied solely on jets of water to create a complex pattern.

After Le Nôtre's death, his pupils continued to modify his techniques: some, such as his nephew Desgotz (who practised extensively in Germany and Sweden) by tackling difficult and asymmetrical sites, others by simplifying his features and increasing the emphasis on views framed along the secondary axes. Ever grander cascades were created, for instance, in Wilhelmshöhe in the early 1700s, and Caserta half a century later. Where the changes in level necessary for cascades were not available, as in the Netherlands, the effect of the water parterre, with or without fountains, was matched by the use of canals (originally serving purposes of

open country; this illusion of penetration into the landscape was reinforced by the absence of apparent walls or fences; boundaries could be effected by the *clair-voyée*, a sunken fence or ditch, later known in England as the ha-ha.

Once the controlling framework was established, the challenge was to integrate as much variety as possible within it. This was the purpose of the various enclosures which were screened from the house and each other by bosquets and hedges. Small sculpture gardens, pools, architectural pavilions of trellis work, areas set aside for games or social pleasures – indeed, all the disparate devices of the Renaissance garden – were included, but the heightened opposition that earlier designers had maintained between the works of people and

The new, naturalistic look of rockwork in the later eighteenth century: the great boulder at Mortefontaine. From Labord, 'Descriptions des Nouveaux Jardins de la France', 1808.

drainage) to flank the main body of the garden.

Submission to Nature

Theories which suggested that the human mind was passive, merely the receiver of impulses and directions from its environment, spread throughout Europe in the eighteenth century. Aesthetic theorists separated the different types of emotional experience – the beautiful, the melancholy, the sentimental, and so on – and asserted that each of these experiences was an inevitable response to certain given stimuli. It followed that each of these responses could be prompted by introducing different features into the garden. Evergreens, perhaps surrounding a tomb, would induce melancholy; rugged rocks would suggest sublime awe; rustic imitations of labourers' cottages would arouse feelings of sympathy and benevolence; flower gardens, delight.

The different kinds of garden buildings and scenic spectacles, which in Le Nôtre's hands would have been integrated within the overall composition, were, in the 1720s, being isolated in glades or at the further removes of promenades, so that they could inspire the appropriate mood within the spectator without fear of competition from adjoining stimuli of a contrasting nature. Thoughts of virtue and nobility could be induced by classical temples; the curiosity value of exotic countries was evoked by temples or bridges in an imitation Chinese style, first used at Versailles in the 1670s, but increasingly popular from the 1730s.

Ten years later, historical reverie was being promoted by artificial ruins in a variety of styles, including the Gothic. As no one knew much more than the superficial about Gothic and non-European architecture, there was no need to aim for accuracy in detail. What were later to become important styles, such as these Greek and Gothic revivals, first appeared in garden buildings; their unconventionality was more tolerable in private estates than in public buildings. The 1740s even saw a reappearance of automata, enacting scenes of peasant life, in the garden of the exiled Polish King Stanislaus at Lunéville.

These developments represented a general loosening-up of the garden of Le Nôtre's day – the tightly controlled plan was being abandoned, and the component parts of the garden scattered. Sometimes, especially in Europe, the number of disparate buildings overcame the 'scatter' principle, and resulted in a jarring clutter. In England, however, a further consequence of the new aesthetic was an organizing principle that helped to keep these various elements, in Pope's words,

> Not Chaos-like together crush'd and bruis'd,
> But as the World, harmoniously confus'd.

This was the ideal of subservience to Nature. First of all, major axes and vistas sweeping from the house were broken up, to suggest an overall openness to the environment; the accepted replacement was a circuitous carriage drive winding through the grounds, and the house was being sited on a downward slope instead of at the top of a hill. The distribution of objects and eye-catchers became increasingly asymmetrical, the curved line was adopted as a standard for beauty, and there were views over open country –

The English landscape style on a comparatively small site: Arno's Grove, north of London.

unobstructed because of the use of the ha-ha – on all sides, not merely down selected vistas. Utilitarian structures, such as walled kitchen gardens, were moved further away into the grounds, out of sight of the house. However, sporadic attempts, from the 1730s, to create *fermes ornées* (ornamental farms) – in which cornfields and grazing land were interspersed with flower borders in an informal landscape – were never successful agriculturally.

The climax of this development came in the 1750s in England with the work of Lancelot Brown, nicknamed 'Capability' for his habit of assessing a property's capabilities for his proposed alterations. His gardens represented a maximum of ease of adaptation to the environment, composed as they were of a very few elements: the lawn, which was brought right up to the house; clumps of trees scattered irregularly; gently undulating ground; surrounding belts of trees which gave uniformity to the prospect; serpentine lakes. The works involved major upheavals: the removal of terraces and avenues, remodelling of landforms, and damming of streams.

The English garden abroad: the gardens of Monte Pincio, Rome, at the beginning of the nineteenth century.

The survival of the flower garden: Sir William Chambers' setting for the aviary at Kew in the 1760s.

Brown's total landscaping served as the model for innumerable 'English gardens' designed throughout Europe in the later eighteenth and first half of the nineteenth century. Nonetheless, it represented only one mood of the eighteenth-century garden, and some of Brown's critics – most notably William Chambers, who began the landscaping of Kew Gardens in the 1750s – objected to the narrow range of effects he offered. Chambers, reasserting the importance of inducing a variety of emotional responses within the garden, invoked Chinese gardens as a precedent; his descriptions owed more to his imagination than to the observation of genuine Chinese gardens, but enough people were convinced for the phrase *'jardin anglo-chinois'* to be adopted in France.

Chambers and some of his contemporaries were particularly concerned to cultivate the sublime: this was the furthest reach of psychological subjection to the environment, entailing the contemplation of scenes that overpowered the imagination with terror or horror. A certain degree of sublimity could be captured from the brutally simple forms of primitive building

– imitation Stonehenges, for example – but in Europe more extreme effects were created, using scenes of darkness, jagged rocks, caves and dead trees. At Hohenheim, in the 1770s, ruins and crude buildings were mixed to suggest the degenerate life of the Dark Ages amid the remains of a former civilization.

By the end of the century, the Brownian park began to be criticized on another level. Brown had justified his landscapes by invoking Nature – but it was a highly idealized and comfortable nature. As the English became gradually more familiar with the primeval forests of North America, it became apparent that Brownian nature was highly artificial; indeed, some of his favourite features had been drawn from the relics of agricultural and industrial development in England (serpentine lakes from the creation of multiple millraces for water power, the alternation of trees and lawn from the enclosure of common land and the use of trees as boundary markers). It was a short step to propose creating gardens which imitated genuine nature, in its wildness and disorder, and the notion was spread by late eighteenth-century manuals which recommended using landscape paintings as models for garden views. By the 1770s the French philosopher Rousseau had already envisaged a garden in which human beings had no place; and William Gilpin had rejected the idea that a garden could ever be natural enough to be truly picturesque. This kind of theory was welcomed in America, where, right through the nineteenth century, the idea prevailed that an urban park, Olmsted's Central Park in New York, for instance, ought to be a way of bringing wild nature into the city.

Ornamental Horticulture in the Nineteenth Century

It was in England that the cult of Nature had reached its fullest development, and it was there that the reaction began against it, even while the English garden was winning converts abroad. The first major rejection of nature as an ideal was Humphry Repton's declaration, in the first decade of the nineteenth century, that 'The garden is a work of art, not of nature'; and from about 1800 Repton was busy reintroducing the formal features, including flower-beds and trellis-work, that Brown had swept away. Thirty years later, largely as a result of the writings of John Claudius Loudon and the head gardeners who contributed to his *Gardener's Magazine*, Repton's slogan had been elaborated into a consistent philosophy.

First of all, it was realized that the eighteenth-century designers had been following not nature, but an *idea* of nature that was the creation of their own imaginations, and therefore artificial; since all garden-making was inevitably artificial, the new aesthetic demanded that it should be seen to be artificial, and the attempt to deceive the spectator into thinking it was a work of nature was declared to be in bad taste. Secondly, it had become apparent that the eighteenth century's attempt to dictate emotional responses to specific garden features was a failure; the mind was not as passive as had been thought, and it was always possible to laugh in the melancholy glade or be bored by the intended surprise. Since the spectator could not be compelled to react one way rather than another, it followed that individuality of response should be encouraged. The new philosophy held up the ideal of the creative imagination. Originality in the design and decoration of gardens became the new presiding value.

The most obvious example of artificiality in the garden is, of course, the greenhouse, and by the 1820s the conservatory was becoming an indispensable ornament to any park or garden. 'Artificial climate' was the watchword in these early days, conjuring up visions of glass ranges in which

How to train fruit trees: Nicolas Gaucher, c. 1900.

every climate of the world, with its accompanying flora, would be represented. Outside the glasshouse, the simplest way of achieving artifice was by planting in tubs instead of in the ground, but one of the most spectacular methods was by planting exotic plants, that no one familiar with the local flora could suppose had grown there unaided. The unlucky owner of a Brownian park could redeem it with the necessary artistic touch, merely by adding a few monkey-puzzle trees or wellingtonias to the grounds. And once again, the garden could be subdivided into areas, each devoted to a different category of plant: the American garden (for peat-loving shrubs), the heathery, the alpine rockery, the fernery.

These customs had become established in varying degrees in England by the 1820s. During the next two decades, English head gardeners developed the bedding system, the most complex use of exotics. This involved changing the contents of flower-beds seasonally, and during the summer using tender and half-hardy exotics which had to be protected under glass in winter. Great attention was lavished on the choice of colour schemes; long borders could be arranged in a series of tints gently shading into each other, but formal beds for public display were planted with a view to high contrast of colour. By the 1850s individual beds were being filled with patterns using different types of plants.

Continental thinking, however, continued to be dominated by the English landscape park until after the mid-century, and the new tendencies were admitted only gradually, and only where they could be accommodated without disrupting the landscape framework. When formal flower-bedding was carried out in France, the vivid contrasts of English colouring were replaced with graded tonal sequences of 'warm' or 'cold' colours, with white flowers

Topiary and exotic conifers on the Hunnewell estate in Massachusetts in the 1890s: the artifice of the Victorian garden.

used as a link between successive tones. The colour theorist Chevreul, who devised this system, argued that it would induce certain emotional reactions in the spectator – an echo of eighteenth-century theory. The idea met with a poor welcome in England until Gertrude Jekyll popularized Chevreul's colour schemes in the herbaceous border at the end of the century. The new Paris parks developed by Alphand in the 1850s and 1860s, still essentially English landscape gardens, made much use of simple, unpatterned flower-beds, supplemented by beds of ornamental-leaved plants, patches of naturalized bulbs, and informal masses of flowers accompanying rockworks. This 'picturesque' planting was promoted by a faction in England during the 1860s, centring around Robert Marnock of Regent's Park and later his protégé William Robinson, whose 'wild garden' was a translation of this French style into England. French and German gardeners made a distinctive contribution to the aesthetic of artifice in the use of deception as a theme in garden ornaments, using one material to imitate the appearance of another, most notably in rustic 'woodwork' executed in concrete or iron.

About 1870, English bedding was augmented by the introduction of carpet bedding – the use of dwarf foliage plants which could be trained into uniform flat surfaces. The reaction against the landscape park was beginning on the Continent, and the full panoply of bedding, carpet and otherwise, was adopted internationally by the end of the decade. These new carpeting techniques encouraged a wide range of fanciful shapes: butterflies, snakes, lettering, portraits, even (in Italy)

A view in the Frankfurt Palmengarten in the 1890s, showing the popularity of carpet-bedding: patterns created with dwarf foliage plants.

Biblical scenes. By the late 1880s, experiments were being made in the use of carpet bedding on three-dimensional frames, to create vases, crowns and human figures.

A final mode of artifice came to fruition in the last quarter of the century, although there had been sporadic attempts as early as the 1820s to create imitations of foreign landscapes, with the characteristic flora. Rock gardens were fashioned as scale models of alpine ranges; Mediterranean gardens, such as the Villa Thuret at Antibes, boasted collections of American cacti; rhododendron forests on the Himalayan model were planted from Cragside in Northumberland to the Villa Carlotta on Lake Como. The turn of the century saw widespread attempts to imitate Japanese gardens – the last-discovered category of exotic landscape – often created by genuine Japanese gardeners, and the large Oriental population in North America ensured that these gardens remained popular there after the fashion had passed in Europe.

Historic Revivals

The new emphasis on artificiality brought with it a new appreciation of the formal or geometrical features that had been swept away by Brown and his contemporaries. Already, in the first decade of the nineteenth century, there were attempts at rehabilitating such older gardens which still survived (one was at Levens Hall, Cumbria, where the topiary was re-cut after 1804), and at creating new terraced gardens where older ones had been (as at Wilton House, Wiltshire).

For the first time, the garden designer had a variety of contrasting styles to choose from. Previously, new movements in gardening had generally been proclaimed as the establishment of the true system, as against the false ideas that had prevailed

before. But, now that a variety of response was encouraged, gardeners were discovering that it was possible to look at earlier types of design, not as right or wrong by some absolute standard, but as styles, each appropriate to its time, and each judged by its own rules. Awakening nationalism led to the categorizing of styles on a national basis, as French, Dutch, Italian – all of which were worthy of emulation, even within different parts of the same garden.

In England the favoured models were Italian gardens of the sixteenth century – popularized by Charles Barry in such gardens as Trentham Park, Staffordshire, and Harewood House, Yorkshire – and French gardens of the late seventeenth century, as shown in W. A. Nesfield's elaborate parterres and Joseph Paxton's attempt to rival Versailles in Crystal Palace Park. There was felt to be no contradiction between using a period pattern, and stocking it with the most recently introduced plants; indeed, the bedding system may have been in part a revival of the change-bedding of Louis XIV.

The first attempts, in the 1840s, at reconstructions which were historically accurate in their planting as well as their design were limited to topiary and herbaceous borders based on a seventeenth-century model. Later in the century, especially after the novel patterns of carpet bedding had opened a rift between historians and experimental horticulturists, there was an increasing move towards the use of 'old-fashioned' flowers (those with medieval or seventeenth-century associations).

The early proponents of carpet bedding in France saw a return to the spirit of Le Nôtre in the mere fact of creating patterned flower-beds; and the double movement, of restoration and imitation, began. Vaux-le-Vicomte was restored in the 1880s by Henri

W. A. Nesfield's nineteenth-century Renaissance-style garden at Witley Court, Herefordshire.

Duchêne and his son Achille, who became the most famous of several designers working in the Le Nôtre mode. Earlier phases of French gardening were also drawn upon, as at Villandry, where a sixteenth-century-style garden was created in the first decade of this century. By that time, the same pattern was emerging in Italy. Before the First World War, Giacomo Boni was urging the importance of historical accuracy of

The Renaissance style around 1900: George Gould's garden at Georgian Court, Lakewood, New Jersey.

planting for excavated Roman sites; and the reconstruction of Renaissance villa gardens began at least as early as 1909, with work on the Castello Balduino, and continued between the wars with such reconstructions as Castelgandolfo.

The diverse national styles gradually turned into a search for historical roots, and made possible international movements in revivalism. The beginning of the twentieth century saw the creation of Renaissance Italian gardens on the grand scale at Hever Castle in Kent, for example, and the Villa Vizcaya in Florida. Some designers, notably Duchêne and J. C. F. Forestier, sought to push the search back to Islamic precedents, creating a Spanish style that spread through America and the Mediterranean countries by the 1920s; others, such as the brothers Vera in France, moved in the direction of pure abstraction, loosely said to be in the Le Nôtre spirit, but, with its mirrored walls and illusions of perspective, more akin to the Art Deco movement. In England where the revivals had begun, interest was increasingly channelled into an attempt to isolate the quintessentially English style. The early decades of this century saw the revival of herb gardening and the creation of the Shakespeare Garden at Stratford-upon-Avon. In a series of gardens, including Mellerstain (the 1900s) and Anglesey Abbey (thirty years later), the experiments of the early landscape gardeners such as William Kent were revived: ironically, historical revivalism ended by restoring the very style against which it had originally reacted.

The Development of the Small Garden
Until very recently, there was not a distinct tradition, either of design or of planting, for the small urban or suburban garden. The earliest urban gardens were those

belonging to religious houses, devoted to food and medicinal plants. Domestic gardens did not become significant until the seventeenth century. Then, the centralization of the state in many European countries meant that the nobility maintained residences in the capitals, in addition to their country estates. These smaller town gardens followed the model of the greater ones within the limitations of scale, but often with a time-lag, so that the suburban estate might embody the values of a previous generation of country-house designers. For instance, it was obviously impractical to attempt a Brownian effect in the grounds of a London house, so that the tradition of 'formal' gardening had continued near, and in, the city.

The nineteenth century saw the sudden growth of the English suburbs, as the villas of the wealthier middle classes spread out from the city. Such villas were characterized by a modified landscape style, using serpentine lines and clumps or specimen trees on a lawn, and gradually adopting the latest experiments in bedding. In America, where the ready availability of land encouraged rows of detached, rather than connected, houses, a similar style was adopted for the front gardens, which were often united into a continuous sequence of partially interrupted lawn running the

A suburban garden of the 1880s – 'The Ivies', in North London – showing carpet bedding and a conifer collection.

length of the street, while back gardens were enclosed and individualized. Anglo-American ideas of decentralized planning spread to Europe late in the nineteenth century, with a resulting suburban expansion; but there, a much greater use was made of fruit gardening as both an ornamental and a practical device. The English maintained a more rigid demarcation between the ornamental and the utilitarian; there was a different emphasis in England and France on food gardening in urban areas. In England, the historical revivalist 'Arts and Crafts' movement called for a return to communal allotments, whereby householders and tenants would lease portions of a plot of land away from their dwellings, and grow fruit and vegetables there. In France, after the Revolution, commercial food had been cultivated on small sites, using techniques pioneered by Louis XIV's kitchen gardener La Quintinye: the ground would be made fertile with imported topsoil, and every available inch put to use by employing masses of cloches and frames. This system, called *culture maraîchère*, was imported into England at the turn of this century as 'French gardening'.

By this century, and the arrival of the garden city, the informally landscaped villa was giving way to formal schemes based on the currently fashionable historical revivals in each country. During the Edwardian period in England especially, the idea, which had long been practised in North America, was developed of the small garden as a source of tranquillity and sentiment rather than stimulation. Such a garden would provide psychological privacy by enclosure, variety by division into compartments (scale permitting), a feeling of closeness to nature by seasonal plantings of the sort Gertrude Jekyll was popularizing, and thoughts of innocence and relaxation inspired by appropriate statuary. Alternatively, shorn of its more sentimental trappings, this mode could be combined with horticultural revivalism under the name of the 'cottage garden' (its followers often claimed, on debatable evidence, that there was an unbroken tradition of cottage gardens from the seventeenth century). Encouraged by the example of such 1930s gardens as Sissinghurst in Kent, the cottage garden has dominated much small garden making to the present day, although the recent growth of interest in herb gardening has brought with it a revival of knot gardens, in which there is an emphasis on greater authenticity in the use of period features.

2
PRACTICAL DESIGNING

The age and appearance of your house will have a direct bearing on the type of garden you create, so you need information about the building itself. Most houses were built for a particular person or, if part of a speculative development, to appeal to a specific market – small tradesmen, prosperous artisans, rich merchants, and so on. A picture of the first owner can be gained from studying title deeds, street directories and parish registers of the period, which you will be able to find in the local public library, museum or archives. The layout of the house itself, and the small details in which it differs from its neighbours or from the standard layout of houses of that particular period, will help you to build up a picture of the first owners.

In the last hundred years or so the rapid changes of taste and fashion have been clearly recorded in newspapers and magazines, back numbers of which can often be found in reference libraries. If you know the exact date of your house, it is possible to choose the precise colours, patterns and even plants which were in vogue that year, to give a completely authentic touch to your reconstruction.

Some houses have of course been much changed over the centuries and in that case your choice of garden style is wide. In some instances the garden would have been designed when the house was first built and remained unchanged in spite of subsequent alterations. Otherwise, the period when a major reconstruction was undertaken is a likely choice or, if the garden is large, you might create a composition from different periods, as varied as the architecture of the house.

First Steps
Never rush in and tidy up or clear an old garden – vital clues to its past appearance can be lost in the process. The first thing to note carefully is ground levels, for once

The lost pattern of parterres at Lilford Hall, Northants., becomes visible in hot, dry weather.

major level changes have been made they are often retained due to the cost of alteration, however much other details of design and planting may have varied with fashion. Long, broad banks forming one or more sides of a rectangle, found in a garden belonging to a seventeenth- or eighteenth-century house, will certainly be the remains of the raised terraces along which people walked to admire the pattern of the knot garden or parterre on the level ground below. A hot, dry summer, or a winter when a thin coating of snow has just begun to melt, often reveal under grass the lost pattern of flower-beds and gravel walks. Another good time for observation is late evening, when low-lying sunlight throws up the slight inequalities in the grass where it rolls over the camber of paths or into the hollows of beds, which generally sink slightly when grassed over.

Deeper hollows might suggest filled-in pools or other water features and could repay further investigation with fork and trowel to see if part of the old structure remains below ground. Gravel paths frequently vanish under grass or soil washed down from a higher level. Where they are grassed over, a slight camber may suggest their presence, but in any case walk the lines of suspected paths jabbing a garden fork into the ground: if there is a path beneath you will strike a hard bottom consistently at the same depth. Because these paths were solidly constructed, you will only have to kill off the grass or scrape away the accumulated mud and leaves, and then, if appropriate, resurface with a little fresh gravel, to have a path which is as good as new.

Levelled ground in a nineteenth- or twentieth-century garden suggests either a formal feature such as a rose garden or a tennis or croquet lawn. A comparatively long, narrow enclosure backed by hedges or shrubberies is almost certainly the site of a pair of herbaceous borders with a central grass path. Such borders were often edged with bands of stone or brick to make the mowing of the central path easier; these bands may still lie beneath the grass, indicating the width of the original borders.

Take careful note of the existing plants and try to decide what was there as part of the original design, what has been added over the years and what is merely self-sown. Certain trees, particularly Ash (*Fraxinus*), Birch (*Betula*), Sycamore (*Acer pseudoplatanus*), Willow (*Salix*) and Alder (*Alnus*), grow vigorously from seed and reach a considerable size in quite a short time, giving them a deceptive appearance of belonging. Various shrubs seed or layer themselves over a wide area. Both the 'wild' *Rhododendron ponticum* and the Common Laurel (*Prunus laurocerasus*) can create a solid jungle over a whole garden. Other shrubs grow rapidly from suckers, spreading far beyond their intended limits, while some herbaceous plants, left to themselves, can also travel far and conceal much. An advantage of these smotherers is that they tend to cover the surface, making their own humus as they go and preserving the garden features beneath their roots. Trees are more destructive; their roots can cause serious damage to features such as walls, steps and buildings. Clearing must therefore be slow and methodical to ensure that no further damage is done in the process.

Once rubbish and obviously irrelevant material have been removed it is easier to get a clearer idea of the intentions of the layout. Sometimes, shrubs or trees have reverted to the original stock, which is generally far stronger than the plant which was grafted on to it. Over the years 'dwarf' trees, particularly conifers on rock gardens, may grow huge, while other plants may simply outgrow space allotted to them. Decisions must then be made as to what must be removed entirely, what can be cut down and allowed to spring up again from the roots, and what can be incorporated into the restored design.

It is always better to live with a garden for a whole year, getting rid of only the obvious rubbish, before undertaking major clearing. If a worthwhile, rare or valuable plant is in the wrong place and cannot be moved, take cuttings yourself or get a local nursery to take them for you.

Plotting the Site

The site itself is the basic element in any project of garden reconstruction. It will control what you can do, what you should plant and what kind of garden you can make. The first thing to make is a survey of the shape and then a scale drawing.

Initially, find out if there are any plans available. Most site plans which form part of the deeds of house property are too small in scale to be of any use, but sometimes larger-scale town plans are available. These go into considerable detail about the buildings and gardens in a street or area. If the house has been altered recently, the architect may have prepared a plan of all or part of the building, showing adjacent paths, garden walls, manhole covers and other details. Even if it only shows doors, windows and down pipes, it will save you a lot of detailed measuring, but do take one or two check measurements to ensure that the plan was actually carried out as drawn.

If the ground is very extensive or very difficult – for instance, part of a steep hillside – it would be worthwhile, although expensive, to use a professional surveyor. However, making a simple ground-level survey yourself is not difficult.

Investigating the Soil and Climate

Soil and climate – and their interaction – will have the greatest influence on your plan and on the plants you can grow. The garden may have the same amount, and quality, of topsoil all over; one trial hole to ascertain the depth is sometimes sufficient. However, with old houses and gardens it may be wiser to make a separate hole in each significant area or dig them to a regular grid pattern all over the site. If in doubt about the quality of the soil, take small samples from several parts of the garden, numbered for identification, for analysis; this will reveal the soil's pH value (which tells whether the soil is acid or alkaline and therefore what ranges of plants it will grow) and what mineral deficiencies it has. Any significant variations in soil type and, of course, any hidden structures, can be indicated on one of your overlay sheets. Also take note of areas where the water gathers and drains poorly, and those which appear to dry out quickly or to receive very little moisture – in the shelter of buildings, for instance, or under large trees.

Although the general climatic conditions and prevailing wind are likely to be the same over the whole region where you live, every garden has its own microclimate conditioned by the surroundings. Winds can be deflected by hills, trees and buildings so that they frequently blow from an unexpected quarter, down-draughts and even minor whirlwinds can occur in the shadow of tall buildings, and fierce gales may be funnelled between them. The presence of winds or draughts may seriously affect where you can sit and what you can grow, so they must be carefully plotted: as little as 2 or 3 metres (6 or 10 feet) can make all the difference between an exposed and a sheltered situation.

Likewise, areas which are frost pockets and hold the cold air, or where snow and frost remain long after they have left other parts of the garden, will need to be measured and their limits noted. So too will those which are warm and protected, where heat may be reflected by surrounding walls and pavings.

At an early stage you should think about sunlight, both in summer and winter: you should plot the movement of the sunlight over your ground at both mid-summer and mid-winter. Generally the line will describe a regular curve across your land, much wider at the high than the low season, of course.

To determine when a feature will receive sun, imagine it positioned at the centre of this wheel, orientated to north. Sun will fall on those aspects facing the sun arc.

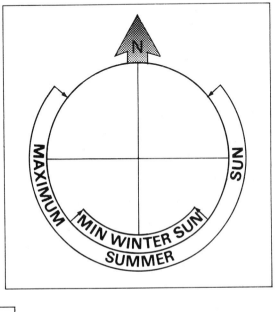

Making a Plan of your Garden

The equipment you will need to make a plan of your house and garden is simple. Buy, borrow or hire two 30-metre (100-feet) measures. (Nowadays it is often possible to hire things which you will need to use for only a short time.) An ordinary metal skewer, fixed to the end of the tape, and stuck firmly into the ground or a convenient crevice in a wall or paving, allows one person to take several measurements from one position by simply moving the free end. Squared or lined paper to keep your lines straight and angles true, a drawing board (a clean pastry board will do), drawing pins and a medium-soft pencil are the other essentials.

Measuring your Garden

Start with a simple drawing of the site – or a part if the whole is large – writing in clearly the important measurements and trying to keep the general proportions true – for instance, the width of the garden in relation to its length.

Decide on your base line: most measurements will be taken from this and everything will relate to it. Ideally this line should extend right through the total area to be surveyed. A boundary wall or fence is best, but if obstructed by existing trees or shrubs, a line must be laid down and pegged out with cord on the ground. In this case, it might be convenient to choose a diagonal rather than a line running across or the length of the ground:

Mark this base line on your drawing: measure it working away from the house, and mark significant points (for future measurements) with pegs. Next take a measurement out from the base line – if using the longest boundary as a base, choose the shorter boundary which appears to meet the base at right angles (check the angle). These two lines make two sides of a triangle: the third, the next line to measure, is the distance between the free ends of the two existing lines. Fix the remaining boundaries by creating another triangle – or a series of triangles if the garden is an irregular shape – from the base line.

The position of features close to the boundaries or actually on lines forming the sides of triangles can be marked in when these main lines are measured. Other objects which lie inside the site – such as trees, groups of

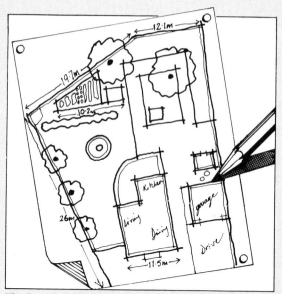

The first stage in drawing up a plan of your site is to make a rough sketch, writing in important measurements and keeping proportions true.

Triangulation

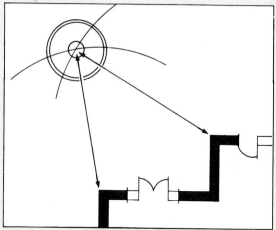

Features difficult to position from the baseline can be plotted by taking two measurements from points already fixed such as house corners. Transfer the dimensions to the plan with a compass, making intersecting arcs to plot the position.

shrubs, manhole covers and permanent features which have to be incorporated into the new design – are measured by a series of small separate triangles. The intermediate measurements already marked with pegs on the base line are used for this: they form known

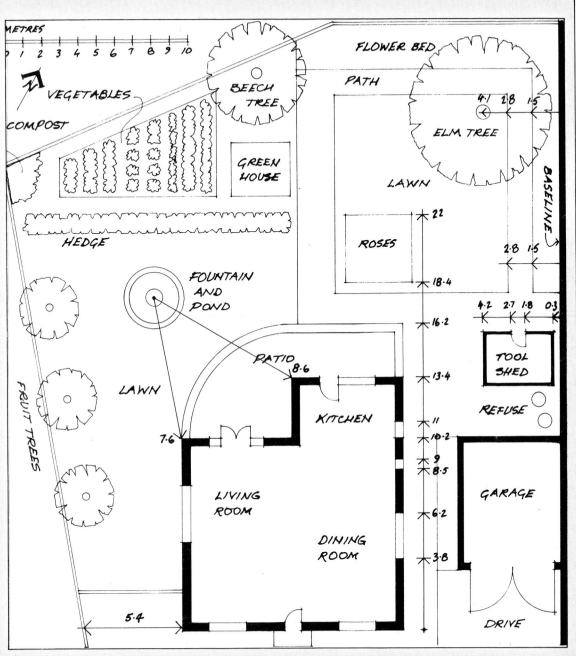

When you have plotted all the information accurately, use tracing paper overlays to try out design ideas.

points of reference from which the small triangles can be measured. Although these smaller triangles may be linked together, they must always be tied back to the base line.

When dealing with features – such as drives or paths – which cannot be altered, you can put in marking pegs either at both ends if they are straight, or at all important changes of direction if they are curved, and then triangulate to those points in the same way as children produce pictures by joining dots together. The other method is to run a single line from one end to the other of the path, fix its position on plan, and then take right-angled offsets from it at regular intervals to both sides of the path. This method is useful when dealing with a curving feature of involved shape, needing a large number of points to permit accurate plotting.

Lastly there are the details of the house itself. You will probably find it easier to take these on a separate sheet, as a large number of detailed measurements will be involved. If you began your garden survey from a corner of the house, then start there. If not, take the corner with the most unrestricted run along the face of the building. Work from one end to the other, noting the measurements to the outer face of each window frame and doorway and the height of window sills above ground level (you will not be able to plot those heights on the plan unless you also decide to draw elevations of the house, but keep it in note form in any case; it is very useful information to have when making your eventual design). Also measure the width, number and height of any steps, the position of drain pipes, manhole covers and gullies, and slabs of concrete which are too solid to remove.

Where there are projections or recesses you will need to measure them separately and either triangulate back from the projecting corners to the main corners of the house, or work the interior of a recess as two triangles. The reason for this is that many old buildings have few walls at right angles to one another, and the cumulative effect of a number of minor differences of angle can result in a very inaccurate plan when it is drawn up. If you have not already done so during the site survey, it is always wise to take a check measurement from corner to corner of the house to ensure that there is not a similar cumulative build up of small errors of measurement between one feature and the next.

Drawing up the Plan

All this information must be drawn to scale accurately. It is best to use graph paper, which not only has a grid of vertical and horizontal lines to work against, but also provides an immediate scale reference. Pin the paper to a large drawing board or old table top.

For the scale – that is, the size that each metre measured on the ground will appear on paper – always use a standard unit which can be measured with a ruler (usually referred to as a 'scale' for drawing purposes). For detailed plans of courtyards, small gardens or areas round the house, a scale of 1:50 is a convenient measurement. At a later stage, when you may be preparing planting plans for particular beds, it is again useful; but for an overall plan or plans of larger areas, 1:100 is more suitable.

Draw in the base line at the appropriate place and mark on the intermediate measurements which you may have taken along it. For the next stage you will need a pair of compasses with an extending arm long enough to cover the longest side of any of your triangles. Measure the other two sides of your first triangle and strike off the two arcs with your compass: the point where they bisect is the position of your first measurement. As each triangle relates to one or more others, you can work on from triangle to triangle, drawing in only the information which has to be shown on the plan. It is not necessary to draw in the sides of the triangles (unless they represent actual lines on the ground) because it is only the points where the arcs bisect which are important. In this way all the remaining triangles can be plotted, the lines of the various features drawn in and detached points – such as the position of an individual tree – named. Lastly the full details of the house with its various projections and recesses, doors, windows and steps can be filled in on the plain block which represented the general bulk of the house in the early part of the survey.

But the garden is most probably not flat. In order to present a clear picture of the ground, you must be able to indicate those vital changes in level on the paper. If the levels are very complicated it might be better to hire a surveyor to do this part of the work for you. The height of the damp-proof course of the building above existing ground level is an essential piece of information if you are contemplating a raised terrace, as it must always be at least 15 cm (6 inches) above finished ground level. (Many old houses have no damp-proof course, in which case it is unwise to raise the level of the ground any higher against the wall. If the building is at all damp, you may need to lower it.) You should also plot the height of any steps on the plan, and any changes in level where sloping ground runs down beside a brick wall, exposing further courses of bricks as the ground level sinks.

Outside your Boundaries

Now consider those factors which lie outside your site but which may have an important bearing on your final design. There may be a view. If you are very fortunate it may be spectacular, or it may merely be pleasant, but in any case it will be seen more easily from some parts of the site than others. The places from which the view may be seen must be carefully noted down and the exact angle of the view shown. This will affect the placing of seats, the flow of paths and the arrangement of terraces.

Sometimes the most interesting features are less obvious: a romantic group of nineteenth-century chimneys and gables seen in silhouette against the sky, an interesting glimpse between city buildings, or an attractive tree in an adjoining garden are all features which, if cleverly emphasized, can be used to draw the eye beyond the immediate boundaries and make the site seem larger than it is. Conversely, there may well be places where planting is needed to hide or at least reduce the impact of unattractive features. All these things should be noted down, as should the areas dominated by neighbours' windows and those which are relatively private.

The presence or absence of these outside factors affects the whole character of your garden: they should influence whether your designing will be extrovert – depending for at least part of its effect on features beyond the boundaries – or introvert and containing all the interest within itself. Such basic decisions, taken at the outset of a garden re-creation project, are essential if the garden is to have a sense of underlying purpose. Without them, it may become merely an aimless collection of period incidents.

The Design

In chapter 1 we saw how garden design has changed, with styles being evolved, discarded and reintroduced over a period of some 500 years. For the practical designer, all these gardens fall into three main types – the pleasance, the formal garden and the informal or romantic garden – and although the style and age of your house must affect the final design, it may be possible to find a variation of the main theme which is related to the building. Gardens, after all, were not always developed at the same time as the house, and in country areas fashions in building and gardening changed slowly, so that a certain amount of leeway is possible in a period reconstruction.

Remember that a single feature, such as a rose garden or a grotto and its immediate surrounds, can be taken from the plan of a large garden and used as the complete design for a much smaller area, adapted if necessary to the shape of the site. But you must be careful not to choose a scheme too elaborate for the nature of the house to which the garden belongs, or the resulting effect will be pretentious.

The Pleasance

Early gardens were very simple, formalized enclosures containing herbs, fruit and flowers grown together in a 'cottage garden' jumble with no attempt at any particular decorative effect. While few medieval houses survive, the general form of small enclosed gardens remained constant for a long period, becoming gradually more elaborate. Such gardens were often shown in paintings and illuminated manuscripts of the fifteenth and sixteenth centuries as a background viewed through a window, or as a bird's-eye perspective. Museums, art galleries and books on the

(opposite) Internal gates between the sections of a garden help to increase the sense of mystery and seclusion. In this case the gates were originally of wooden trellis-work, an idea copied from the illustrations for children's books painted by Kate Greenaway in the early years of this century. Inevitably these rotted in time and they have been replaced by gates of wrought iron, whose repeating curved pattern echoes the curved ends of the adjoining yew hedges. This area was once the children's garden, complete with play house, sand pit, swing and box edged plots for individual gardening.With the family grown up and scattered, the enclosure has become a garden of lilies and camellias.

(opposite, left) A slope which falls across the main line of sight from the house has a very disquieting impression. Wherever possible it should be terraced to create level areas, either formally, using retaining walls and steps, or informally, with banks and groups of shrubs on the lower side to provide a buttressed effect. In this case neither solution was practical. Fortunately a bold sculpture with its strong diagonal movement in the opposite direction was found to provide the necessary counterpoise.

(above) The basis for this small hedged garden was actually a derelict Victorian greenhouse. Once the superstructure was removed the low walls were retained to hold a structure for climbing roses and the old water tank at the end was filled in to make a raised platform for a piece of sculpture. A brick pattern with a framework of old York stone makes a simple parterre in the centre, planted with low foliage plants round a stone urn.

(opposite, right) In this country garden the swimming pool was relegated to a remote part of the orchard. As it was built on an upper level the pool itself was not visible, and a striking effect has been obtained by cutting a narrow tunnel through an old Victorian shrubbery to reveal the terrace steps and a group of white-painted, nineteenth-century iron furniture in a distant patch of sunlight. Looking from light through darkness to light again adds an element of drama and depth to an otherwise ordinary scene, and can be used to make a small area appear much larger.

history of garden design will provide examples. A town house dating, even in part, from the sixteenth or early seventeenth century, or a small country house built as late as the end of the seventeenth century, could have a garden of this type.

The first essential of the pleasance garden is a sense of enclosure and security. Frequently, a wall of brick or stone surrounded the whole garden with internal subdivisions made of slighter materials, but such walls would be very costly to reproduce today. However, it is worth looking at modern materials which recreate a period feel; concrete blocks, for example, rendered with cement and painted white could give the effect of the startlingly white stone walls shown in some paintings. But to retain their effect, they would need to be repainted fairly frequently, thus posing a constant problem of maintenance.

If a wall is too ambitious, there are several other forms of enclosure which are suitable: fences of close-set palings, each pale having a sharply pointed top, were sometimes used, and in simple country gardens wattle hurdles. Although initially cheap, wattle needs frequent replacement and is not a good choice for permanent effect, but may be used as a temporary screen until a boundary hedge has grown up. Since the purpose of these boundaries was to exclude marauders and stray animals, outer hedges were generally of Quick Thorn (*Crataegus monogyna*), sometimes mixed with Sweet Briar (*Rosa rubiginosa*), or of Holly (*Ilex aquifolium*), and were both high and thick for maximum protection.

Within the garden there were often internal divisions of a much slighter kind. Trellis-work was, at first, made from light stakes tied together, and later developed into elaborate 'carpenters' work', with neat panels of laths framed in timber. These screens were often planted with red and white roses, Honeysuckle (*Lonicera periclymenum*), Hops (*Humulus lupulus*) or fruiting Vines (*Vitis vinifera*), while at other times the woodwork was left unplanted. In paintings, the climbers appear to be very sparse, clearly showing the structure beneath, but whether this was the intended effect or an artist's convention, it is hard to tell. Other forms of division were roses trained to poles stuck in the ground to form a thin screen, trained fruit trees similar to the modern espalier or cordon, and wattle fences.

Carpenters' work was also used for covered walks, similar to the modern pergola but generally with a semi-circular rather than a flat top. Many of these walks were quite elaborate with carved wooden pillars set on bases of stone, the arched roofs being formed from squared trellises bent to shape over curved braces.

Often, the flower-beds had small trellis fence surrounds, or low edgings of wattle which must have been worked on the spot, using supple withes of Willow (probably *Salix viminalis*) or Hazel (*Corylus avellana*). From records and contemporary accounts it seems that much of the trellis-work was painted, rather than stained.

The beds themselves were generally square or oblong, arranged in a simple chequered pattern, and frequently had, as a centre-piece, a small standard shrub or a plant trained round a framework of wooden hoops. In a modern reproduction garden, a standard currant or gooseberry, a clipped Bay tree (*Laurus nobilis*) or an upright Rosemary (*Rosmarinus officinalis* 'Miss Jessup') make practical substitutes. In the earlier gardens some of these compartments were planted with vegetables, others with a mixture of flowers and herbs – and occasionally with a single type of flower, such as roses or carnations. Later, these beds were turned into knot gardens.

One curious feature of this type of garden was the turf seat, a raised bed retained generally by brick walls and planted with grass to form a bench. The mount was the other major element of these gardens. This was a formalized artificial hill, sometimes in the centre of the garden or at one corner, from which one could not only admire the pattern of the knots but also see over the boundaries to the country beyond.

Water in these early gardens generally consisted of a modest square or circular pond edged with brick or stone set flush with the ground. From this flowed a narrow channel, similarly edged, carrying away the water which was fed in by an elaborate fountain. Almost all illustrations show this feature as being outsize in relation to the pond and of an eccentric appearance, misusing classical motifs. The only way to reproduce an effect of this kind would be to buy odd sections of old carved stonework and create an individual piece for yourself. Or follow the other theme of these gardens and have an apparently natural spring bubbling up from the depths of the pool.

Usefulness and 'curiosity' were the qualities most desired in plants, rather than size or brilliance of flower. In the larger, later gardens containing several enclosures, one was often devoted to an orchard of fruit trees growing in grass, filled with wild flowers – a style which is popular again now.

With the growing influence of the formal garden, the purely domestic pleasance declined in popularity. Certainly many curious and useful plants survived in cottage gardens until the late nineteenth and early twentieth centuries, when a new form of

Twentieth-century pleasance gardens used vernacular materials, as in this Lutyens brick pergola at Hestercombe.

The sixteenth-century reconstruction at Bruges shows the symmetrical beds and formal topiary typical of the period.

pleasance developed as a setting for the 'Arts and Crafts' movement houses. Their gardens, like the houses, used the same local materials for walls, steps and pavings and borrowed from earlier gardens the water tanks, stone-edged channels, borders supported by low retaining walls, trained trees, arbours, box-edged beds and simple topiary.

The planting was no longer a collection of the rare, curious or useful, but consisted of picturesque groupings in which form, texture and colour were combined in a manner derived from the Impressionist painters. And the palette was very rich, for in the intervening centuries a vast number of new hardy plants had been introduced which were now used with a lavish hand in bold drifts and swathes of subtle colour.

This movement is well documented in books and many of the gardens still exist. It is very important to remember the vernacular basis of this work and to use local materials according to local methods of construction.

The Formal Garden

The formal, symmetrical garden was a product of the Italian Renaissance. From the gardens of Italy came balustrades, elaborate seats and architectural embellishments of steps, terraces and pavilions. The emphasis was on the structure of the garden, and walls became the background for beautifully trained fruit trees. Hedges, mainly of Yew (*Taxus baccata*) or Holly (*Ilex aquifolium*), were cut into architectural shapes and these two plants, together with

The water parterre at Villa Gamberaia near Florence shows the importance of topiary in the formal garden.

Box (*Buxus sempervirens*), were trimmed to form the topiary pieces which were so popular at the time.

Not all hedges were evergreen, and Beech (*Fagus sylvatica*) and Hornbeam (*Carpinus betulus*) were popular. As an alternative to topiary, fruit trees trained into equally fanciful shapes, such as lyres, hearts, globes and crowns, were also used, especially in France. Cordons were trained over arches, either to emphasize a crossing of paths or to create the long shady tunnel walks which replaced the galleries of carpenters' work of the earlier gardens.

Another form of green architecture was created by pleaching, a system of training trees – generally varieties of Lime (*Tilia*) or Hornbeam (*Carpinus betulus*) – still particularly favoured in European gardens. The principle is the same as that of the espalier fruit trees in the kitchen garden, only standard trees were used to form a tall screen above a wall, or to make a living pergola or garden house.

Circular basins with fountains or long canals of still water were very much a feature of these gardens, creating a calm reflective feeling. Water plants, so popular in the early twentieth century, had no part in these schemes, although underwater oxygenators and fish kept the water clean and pure. Many of the fountain figures, urns and other statuary were of lead. Rather than have an inferior figure or one from the wrong period, a single jet of water rising from the centre of the basin would be perfectly correct and is very easy to achieve.

In the ambitious gardens, parterres with flowing designs in clipped *Buxus semper-virens* 'Suffruticosa' against a background of coloured gravel, crushed brick or stone chippings, replaced the geometrical knots of the previous style. Otherwise the emphasis was on fine grass surrounded and cut into square or oblong shapes by gravel paths. In the centre of each grass plot there was generally a statue, or sometimes a piece of topiary, or a vase filled with flowers, but there was very little other decoration or 'gardening' as we know it. The results were calm, restful, well ordered and – at least in the smaller, less ambitious garden without parterres or elaborate sculpture – rather dull.

Thanks to the fashion for engraving bird's-eye views of country houses, important buildings or even parts of towns, we have plenty of documentary evidence of the appearance of these gardens. A little study with the local archivist, museum or print seller will result in a crop of ideas which can be applied to the garden of any house from the late seventeenth to the late eighteenth centuries.

Almost all these formal gardens were swept away by the followers of the landscape school, but formal styles were revived in the nineteenth century largely through the medium of architecture. These gardens were basically derivative, but to the purity of the old formal garden they added certain elements of their own. Many of the features of Italian Renaissance gardens, together with the numerous urns and statues with which the gardens were furnished, were no longer of stone but of various manufactured materials, including cast iron.

As plants from every region poured into European gardens, parterres were replaced by patterns of flower-beds set in grass or

The formal garden at Ascott, Bucks., is a good example of late nineteenth-century Victorian bedding and topiary.

gravel and filled with brilliant half-hardy flowers which might be changed three times in a season. Such lavish projects are no longer possible, but a permanent planting of subjects with coloured leaves or a long period of flowers, underplanted with bulbs for spring display, makes an acceptable substitute. The straight gravel walks were now edged with borders of flowers and hardy shrubs, while exotic climbers replaced the trained fruit trees of the earlier garden.

Formal gardens of this kind surrounded the villas which were built in ever-increasing numbers for the rising middle class. Contemporary gardening books give many designs for gardens of this kind, together with a great deal of advice on planting which, if adapted to changed conditions, can still apply today.

The last type of formal garden, almost as rare as the seventeenth-century examples because so few were made, is the rigid geometric garden sometimes found as a setting for the Cubist concrete and glass houses of the late 1920s. There was great

A new type of formal garden emerged in the twentieth century as a setting for the Cubist concrete and glass houses of the late 1920s. Edgings, raised plant boxes and pre-cast paving slabs were of concrete, while softer materials such as grass, water or flowers filled in these outlines. Trees were grown in lines or formal groups. This style of garden is easily recreated today as materials are readily available, but care must be taken not to ruin the effect with even the smallest concession to romanticism. (left and below).

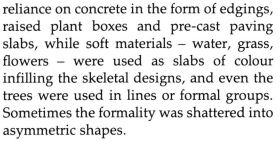

reliance on concrete in the form of edgings, raised plant boxes and pre-cast paving slabs, while soft materials – water, grass, flowers – were used as slabs of colour infilling the skeletal designs, and even the trees were used in lines or formal groups. Sometimes the formality was shattered into asymmetric shapes.

Strangely enough there were far more modernist houses than gardens, and it would be interesting to create suitable period gardens. The basic materials – *in situ* concrete and pre-cast slabs – are readily available and not expensive, while the simple technique of blocks of a single colour or texture in the planting are easy to achieve and maintain. However, great restraint is needed since any hint of romantic overgrowth would destroy the effect. As there are so few authentic gardens, ideas for shapes and colours can best be obtained from paintings of the period, and from contemporary designs for rugs and fabrics.

The Informal or Romantic Garden

The landscape garden is generally thought to be a large-scale composition – more park than garden – of hills, woods, lakes and rivers, decorated with classical temples, ruined towers, grottoes and other conceits, but this style can also be adapted to suit small gardens. Indeed, there were many quite small informal gardens during the 'landscape' period.

The object was to make the garden appear larger than it was, and to achieve this great use was made of contouring and dense planting. Gravel walks led through dells – sometimes revealing a 'romantic' rocky outcrop, which took the place of the ruined castle of the landscape park – to a grotto hollowed from a neighbouring bank, the top planted with trees to make it appear impressive. Grassy glades wound through shallow valleys banked with flowering shrubs to a small lawn with an urn, a seat or perhaps a rustic arbour planted with honeysuckle; and there was great emphasis on sweet scents and flowers.

Word pictures of such 'domestic romantic' gardens appear in novels of the late eighteenth and early nineteenth centuries. Early examples are not well documented in practical gardening books, but if the basic principles of concealment, surprise, variety and seclusion are followed it should not be difficult to create a garden with the right feeling. Generally simple flowers, only one removed from the wild, create a better effect than complex double forms with bright colours, which suggest a much later date. Most of what are referred to as 'cottage garden' flowers would be suitable, but used to more sophisticated effect than in the cottage garden.

There has been a movement in recent years to make excellent reproductions of urns, seats and similar features in reconsti-

The graceful effect of shrub roses in an old garden.

tuted stone, while certain specialist firms build the trellis arbours and covered seats appropriate to these gardens. Whatever decorations are chosen it is important to remember that the makers of these gardens were often people of taste but not necessarily of wealth, so that anything pretentious or obviously costly would be quite out of character.

The wild garden of woodland and flowering meadows is a part of present practice; however, a simple form emerged briefly as a setting for the modernist houses of the 1920s and 1930s. This generally consisted of thin groves of trees, natural or planted (in the latter case, the delicate lines of the Silver Birch [*Betula pendula*] were considered the best) above a carpet of daffodils, through which flowed mown grass glades linking the free-shaped lawns round the house to the recesses of the adjoining woodland, which was carefully thickened with evergreens to hide the boundary. Such designs were considered much more as a link between the lines of the house and the wider landscape, than as gardens in their own right.

3
LAWNS

In her *Ladies' Companion to the Flower Garden*, published in the 1840s, Mrs Loudon wrote: 'Smooth turf, when of any extent in pleasure grounds, is called a lawn; and its chief beauties are the uniformity in the kinds of grasses which cover it and which provide a uniform tone of green.' The definition and requirements remain the same today, in spite of the fact that Mrs Loudon was writing at a time when the mechanical lawn mower was in its infancy.

Because of its regenerative nature and the simple fact that it covers every meadow and hill in the temperate world, there is a general misconception that grass requires scant management. But the primary reason for the success of the British lawn and those in northern Europe, parts of the Southern Hemisphere and the maritime southern states of the North American continent is the climate. One theory is that a regular dew formation on grass during the night does far more to maintain a good green sward than all the labour-intensive and costly devices available; and only in such temperate regions is dew so prolific. In southern Europe – for example, the Mediterranean islands and Madeira – where temperatures do not fluctuate so widely between night and day, the grass is far less lush. Stoloniferous, wide-bladed grasses flourish best in these warmer and drier climates: grasses generally darker in colour, coarser in appearance, slower to regenerate and generally lacking the uniformity of those grasses of which Mrs Loudon wrote.

The Lawn Proper

Areas of maintained turf in England came to be described as 'laund' (later 'lawn') about 1548, and yet it was not until the landscape ideas of the eighteenth century that grass came into its own as an essential part of the garden. By emulating the countryside, with extensive areas of grass, trees and water all contrived and controlled to appear as natural features, England created a style of gardening which came to be

Expanses of grass were an integral part of the landscape garden during the eighteenth century.

known as *le jardin Anglais*. It follows that only in temperate climates can the style be maintained successfully.

The word 'lawn' first came into use about 1733, significantly when set against the history of gardening. The earliest stirrings of the landscape style of gardening were contemporary with its use: the earlier 'laund' had signified a 'stretch of untilled or grass-covered ground'. So it is perhaps permissible to allocate the word 'lawn' quite precisely to mown or shorn grass, and to accept that the vogue developed from the 1730s onwards.

Attempts to sweep away formality and imitate the landscape meant that generally the grass was brought right up to the house, so an uninterrupted view to the horizon could be enjoyed. Visually, the meadows 'belonged', their simplicity contrasting with the highly decorative interiors of the houses. These lawns were cropped by sheep or cut by scythe. The day before scything, heavy rollers were used to consolidate and level the turf. Three skilled mowers could scythe an acre in a day. They worked as a team, advancing together or working from the edge towards the centre, progressing in ever-decreasing rectangles. Sweepers following with birch besoms and rakes collected the trimmings into straight lines. However skilled a worker was, the marks of the cutting blade of the scythe remained in the grass for several days. Between mowings, daisy heads were removed by a daisy rake.

This painting by Balthasar Nebot in 1738 shows the scythes used to cut the grass of the landscape garden lawns.

Grass as a Main Feature

In the early nineteenth century, the Empress Joséphine employed English and French gardeners to make *un jardin Anglais* at Malmaison. Following her lead, other French *parcs* and *plantations* were created, with circuitous walks amid trees, perhaps with a lake and cascades, but always with grass as the main feature: notably at La Motte, Nogentet, Saint Augustine and Courrances. But, outside England, this particular style of gardening has remained most favoured in northern Europe. In Sweden, for example, where summers are light and winters cold and dark, grass appears to survive well, and the woodland-meadow garden is effective. The expanse of lawn at the Palace of Drottningholm is as green and smooth as any in England or Ireland.

There are many remarkable gardens in the south-eastern states of North America, but the two most exceptional were made by famous statesmen: Mount Vernon by George Washington, and Monticello by Thomas Jefferson. George Washington closely followed the styles current in his home state, Virginia, employing master gardeners from England. Apart from the formal areas for the shrubs, flower garden and kitchen garden, he created an extensive bowling green or lawn, dating from 1785, in front of the house, at each side of which was a serpentine walk embellished by trees. At Monticello, Thomas Jefferson was more concerned in forming a *ferme ornée* from 1760 onwards; it contained fewer lawns as such, but both estates were noteworthy for their horticultural practice.

Flowery Meads

Medieval gardens shown by the illuminists and painters of the fourteenth and fifteenth centuries are consistent in portraying a lush meadow-like grassy area bespeckled with flowers. The paintings were symbolic, the paths often forming a cross with a fountain at the centre – the straight paths represent the straight and narrow of a Christian's life; the fountain the eternal fount of life; the flowery mead, the bountiful harmony – and they can be easily copied, in the smallest area. The beds were square or rectangular, edged and supported with wood to encourage drainage, making slightly raised beds. This means that the edges of the turf could be easily kept neat.

Today, there are specialist seed companies producing wild flower and grass combinations, known as conservation mixtures, which when sown provide a rewarding 'meadow'. Ground preparation demands the routine clearing of perennial weeds, surface working and preparation of a good tilth. Details of sowing rates and management normally accompany the seed packages.

Establishing a Lawn

General preparation of the site requires the clearing of perennial weeds, levelling and working the area with a good rake, but the argument has always been alive between seeding or turfing. It appears that methods of turfing have changed little over the years. Between 1890 and 1920 the orthodox size of turf, cut from upland grassland areas, was 91.5 × 30.5 cm (3 × 1 feet) and rolled for handling, or 30.5 cm (1 foot)

Seventeenth-century bowling alley at Bramshill, Hants.

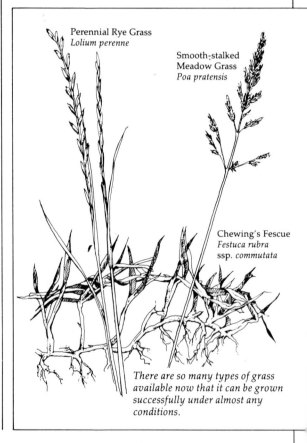

Perennial Rye Grass
Lolium perenne

Smooth-stalked Meadow Grass
Poa pratensis

Chewing's Fescue
Festuca rubra
ssp. *commutata*

There are so many types of grass available now that it can be grown successfully under almost any conditions.

Dandelions, daisies and bluebells create a flowery mead.

Browntop Bent
Agrostis tenuis

Creeping Red Fescue
Festuca rubra
ssp. *rubra*

Zoysia

square handled flat. During the 1930s there was a strong preference for sea-washed turf, a naturally short and even-textured grass.

Lawns were sometimes established by scattering chopped stolons of grass over a prepared surface; various 'crab' grasses were propagated in this way. In Mediterranean countries such vegetative means are still used in preference to seed sowing and the stoloniferous grasses used are generally more ground-hugging, flat-bladed and a darker green than lawn grasses of northern Europe.

In America various regional grasses have been developed, each suited to prevailing soil and climatic conditions. The evaluation of turf grasses was started as early as 1880 at the Michigan Agricultural Experiment Station, and about five years later turf gardens were set up in Connecticut. Other research centres took up the 'grass gardening' call, especially for production of superior sports turf. Lawns, as a feature of both private and public gardens, have remained more important in America, Australasia and Britain than in other countries.

Lawn Maintenance

Shears have been used for cutting or shearing grass and other plants into a reasonably even surface since the thirteenth century, when a rudimentary form of bowls was played. The natural turf was shorn and subsequently swept to achieve a regular surface and, certainly by the fifteenth century, games areas are recorded as being planted with chamomile: this was the surface on which Sir Francis Drake's famous game of bowls (1587) is said to have been played. It is interesting that following legislative control about 1541, all greens had to be licensed and were therefore only privately owned. Bowling became

A Chamomile Lawn

The most suitable type of chamomile for a lawn is the non-flowering form, *Anthemis nobilis* 'Treneague', a clone derived in the 1930s and 1940s; it is evergreen and ground hugging and soon forms a fairly close-woven sward, although it is not as even and hardwearing as grass. To save money, you can buy enough plants to cover just half the area required; the chamomile will provide sufficient cutting material to plant the other half the following season. Spring or early autumn are the best times for planting: the soil is dry enough to be raked level and cleared of perennial weeds.

To cover an area of about 2 square metres (about 2.2 square yards), plant about 100 small plants about 15 cm (6 inches) apart. Stagger the chamomile plants rather than planting them in rows, so that the runners form a closely woven mat. Place the base of the thread-like leaves on the soil, and then press down the ground around the plant. Start in the middle of an area and work outwards, or begin at one side and work right across, moving backwards.

Keep the area moist and, because the growth cannot be mown until it is very well established, it must be weeded by hand. The lawn or pathway may be trodden upon about a month after planting and although it is never going to make a hard-wearing lawn, it will soon provide an apple-scented sitting-out area. Maintain the period effect by cutting with a sickle or bill hook, keeping the swathes even and brushing up the clippings afterwards. Where modern labour-saving cutting devices are used, a hover-type mower gives a better result than a cylindrical blade mower.

Other Scented Lawns

Similar but less decorative lawns can be formed in the same way using clover, pennyroyal, thyme or pearlwort. When thyme is selected use the carpet or mat-forming types rather than hummock-forming plants. Carpet-rooting thymes include *Thymus herba-barona*, the caraway-scented thyme *T. pseudolanuginosus* (which is very hairy and gives a hoary or frosted effect), and *Thymus drucei (T. serpyllum)*. All are evergreen, all flower with tiny lilac-pink flower-heads in high summer, and all need to be set about 30 to 38 cm (12 to 15 inches) apart. Growth is slow. The lawn must be hand weeded for the first couple of years and later, hand clipped in spring and late summer.

A Flowery Mead

Specialist seed companies now produce wild flower and grass combinations, but the best results are likely to be gained by sowing the seeds of wild species that are locally common, as they have already adapted to local conditions. Sow the seeds onto soil that has been carefully raked and weeded and mow the mead, once established, once a year by scythe.

Chamomile makes a lovely apple-scented lawn.

Wild orchids thrive in this flowery mead.

part of Elizabethan garden entertainment, presumably on chamomile or shorn meadow turf, or sometimes on house terraces. The surface would be rolled, shorn, swept and probably rolled again. Rollers were made by boring a hole through a length of felled tree trunk (beech was a favourite), and then inserting a rod and cord to pull it along. Stone rollers were used also, becoming more popular in the early eighteenth century as grass was increasingly cultivated. Some of these were extremely heavy and were therefore horse-drawn.

The art of clipping plants closely at ground level appears to have been practised first by the gardeners caring for knot gardens. Patterns were formed in sweet-smelling plants, almost like carpet designs, at ground level; once the patterns opened out into the formalized open knot, or plat, the close clipping of block-planted sweet-smelling plants continued. Here surely was the rudimentary decorative lawn – chamomile, clover, thyme or pennyroyal spread, carpet-like, on the ground.

Exotic grasses, which are called lawn mixtures of seed today, were known in the Low Countries some time before 1600, but there is no evidence of their use elsewhere until the middle of the seventeenth century. In the mid-seventeenth century ley farming, where some land is kept temporarily under grass, was transformed by new crops of Sainfoin (*Onobrychis sativa*), Trefoil and Clover (species of *Trifolium*), and the introduction of foreign species of grasses stimulated a profound change in grassland management. It was common practice to import grassland turf into 'sports areas' of gardens, where a neatly shorn effect was required.

Lawn maintenance became widespread during the nineteenth century, following

An interesting effect can be created by setting a lawn mower to cut at different heights.

the introduction of the mechanical lawn mower, and then of hoses which would carry water under pressure. The effect and effectiveness of the mechanical lawn mower changed the whole concept of turf maintenance.

The first machine was manufactured in 1831 by Mr Ferabee of Phoenix Works, Stroud, Gloucestershire, to a design by Edwin Beard Budding. It had a cylindrical blade which Budding was accustomed to using for cutting cloth at Brimstone Mills. By the 1850s several designs were patented in North America, and in 1878 the American 'Pennsylvania' side-wheel mower with train-wheel drive was patented in England and put on the English market.

Budding's first mower had a 48-cm (19-inch) cutting blade and was designed to be pushed from the rear, but another handle at the front could be pulled by a second operator. As the lawns of the temperate regions increased in importance and size, their maintenance became a

Summary of lawn types and tools

Medieval period
Grass grown in the flowery mead (a meadow-like grassy area bespeckled with flowers), for turf seats and for bowling alleys. A sickle and scythe were used for maintenance.

Sixteenth century
Grass not yet considered an essential part of the garden. Instead, knot gardens were popular – scented plants shorn near ground level and planted in geometrical or ribbon-like patterns. Gardening implements included sickle, hand shears and scythe.

Seventeenth century
Knot gardens developed into parterres, with more elaborate patterns extending over larger area at the front of the house. Gravels, stones, crushed brick and other materials were used to emphasize the pattern. Main gardening implements were the scythe, sickle, bill hook and hand shears.

Eighteenth century
The landscape movement, in which gardens were planned to emulate the countryside, meant that grass became an essential and decorative part of the garden. Lawns came right up to the house. Intensively maintained by rollers, scythes, daisy rakes and besoms.

Nineteenth century
Lawns increased in size and in importance as a decorative feature. Lawn games became popular: tennis, badminton and croquet. Introduction of the first mechanical lawn mower designed by Edwin Budding in 1831 led to banded, or striped, lawns. Types of mower included man-operated, horse-drawn and steam driven.

Twentieth century
Banded or striped lawns continue to be fashionable until development of hover mower after 1945, which produced a carpet-like effect. Lawn continued to be a major decorative feature and play area, with meticulous care lavished upon it until development of superior mowers and growth regenerative sprays. Mowers included petrol (1902), gang (1914), electric (1919), rotary (1934), and hover (post 1945).

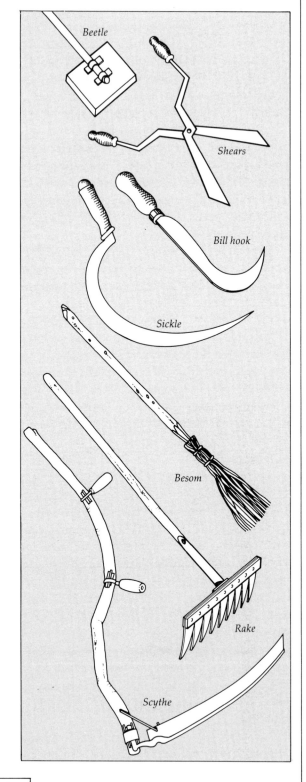

The 'banded' effect of this lawn at Avebury can only be achieved with a cylinder mower.

Areas of rough grass are left to contrast with the smooth lawn at Iford Manor, Wiltshire.

labour-intensive fetish. The first 'five-roller' horse-drawn mower was patented about 1850, while over forty years later, a steam-powered grass-cutting machine was designed: it resembled a river tug and weighed 1.5 tonnes (1½ tons)! The first petrol-powered mowers were manufactured about 1902.

The width of the cutting blades throughout the late nineteenth and early twentieth centuries became wider and wider to cover the large domestic lawns more quickly. The narrow-bladed mowers were reserved for the border edges and grass paths, and were known as border mowers.

The lawn, by now, was skilfully banded or striped by the alternate direction of the cut, as the operator paced the area. The direction was perhaps east to west, then west to east; alternate cuttings would be north to south and south to north to maintain an even sward. Sometimes the banding followed the contour of the site. To produce a pre-Second World War effect, the site needs to be banded in this way, but, because the progress in grass seed mixtures has been considerable, the persistent 'bent' grasses – which were resistant to cylindrical blade mowers – no longer stand up as sentinels after cutting. The breakthrough came with a tough machine, in which the blades spun horizontally, devastating the bent grasses and coping also with rough grass areas.

After 1945 this hover-type mower revolutionized the appearance and texture of lawns everywhere. Not unlike the domestic vacuum cleaner, it coasts over uneven patches, banks, the rough and the smooth, and the operator no longer needs to have a keen eye for a straight line. The lawn is no longer decorated and striped, but is now a rather inferior green carpet. The development of the lawn, as a garden feature, has been reversed.

No one would wish to revert to the early grass-seed mixtures nor to the fantastic Victorian watering machines and lawn sprinklers. So the would-be period garden creator must try to achieve a meticulously striped effect using a cylindrical blade machine: this is what lends the contemporary character to the lawn.

Superior Turfs

As lawn and turf became smoother and more even, so games on grass became more popular. Bowls was revived in Scotland during the nineteenth century, with sea-washed turf often being used for forming the even sward. Scottish immigrants introduced the game to America and the colonies.

The sea-washed turfs, or links, of Scotland were used in the formation of golf courses (hence the name golf links). In the mid-nineteenth century, one company introduced not only lengths of tubing with a union joint every 91.5 metres (100 yards) to provide mobile lawn watering devices, but

also a golf ball. Rubber balls followed in 1902, and it was the Scots again who took the sport to America: The first club was established there at St Andrews, New York, in 1888. As a domestic lawn game, putting developed in both England and America during the Edwardian period.

Tennis

Variations of racquet and ball games developed in France during the twelfth century and by the fourteenth were played exclusively in church cloisters and were called *jeu de paume*. Derived directly from this was the old indoor court game of tennis, or real tennis as it is known today, which has remained more popular in America than in Europe.

Modern lawn tennis evolved from real tennis in the 1860s. At first the court was merely marked out for play on the lawn and the net erected; surrounding ball-confining netting seems not to have been used until around the turn of the century.

Badminton and croquet became lawn games, the latter a development of the medieval French *paille maille*. Croquet proper is said to have been brought from France to Ireland in 1852 and played upon the lawn at Lord Lonsdale's house there.

To create a Victoriana or Edwardian atmosphere, set up croquet or lawn tennis near the house on a lawn with mowing bands formed by a cylindrical blade machine. Have a look for spectators' seats and chairs of the period, which you will find in illustrated catalogues, libraries and museums; and then keep a watchful eye out over junk yards and auction rooms. The seats are uncomfortable but stable. Add stout 'Russian mats' to protect the feet from the dampness of the grass, and serve spectators with tea and cucumber sandwiches to provide the finishing touches.

4
PLANTS
AND PLANTING

The first botanic gardens were established in Italy in the middle of the sixteenth century, and were followed soon afterwards by others at Montpellier, Leyden, Breslau, Heidelberg and Oxford Universities. The Royal Gardens in Paris (established in 1597; later Le Jardin des Plantes) and Leyden University became renowned for their introduction of rare plants.

By 1700, scarcely a ship left France without a botanist on board, while Dutch sea captains received instructions to collect plants and seeds from any port at which their ships might call. While the British East India Company established a botanic garden near Madras for plants from even further east, West Indian and North American species were being introduced to England, where attempts were made to grow the latter out of doors. Notable too, was the introduction to Amsterdam of plants from the Cape of Good Hope in the early years of the eighteenth century, completing a period in which scientific links were forged between the European botanists and private individuals who first formed collections of rare plants.

Climatic Zones
Exotic plants are obviously more suited to some countries than others, and indeed, this applies to different areas within a single country. The Pyrenees and the north of Scotland lie between the northern latitudes of 40° and 60°, which take in virtually the whole of France as well as Germany, Holland, Belgium and the British Isles. Within similar latitudes in North America is a belt across the continent which runs from Philadelphia to northern Labrador; in the Southern Hemisphere the comparable range of latitudes includes some parts of South America, Tasmania and the South Island of New Zealand.

Species from the Southern Hemisphere and North America should, in theory, be interchangeable with each other and those from within similar latitudes in Europe. But in fact the lie of the land, the altitude, rainfall, intensity of light, proximity to the sea, temperature and soil are important factors in the success or failure of establishing exotics out of doors. Hence the British Isles and the coastal strips of North-West Europe, which benefit from the Gulf Stream, have an advantage over continental countries, such as Germany, Holland and France, which are subjected to extremes of heat and cold.

The Royal Botanic Gardens at Kew near London and the area west of Ostend extending to the Pyrenees are part of the same climatic zone, with an oceanic climate of mild winters and cool summers; this reaches across the north of Europe, although it excludes parts of Scandinavia. Ireland, which is even more favoured than Britain, is in a special category; it is in the same zone as Tasmania and the south-east corner of Australia. Plants from the South Island of New Zealand and the regions of high rainfall in Australia flourish in Ireland and similar areas, and those from New Zealand's North Island and other parts of Australia succeed well in the south of England and even better in the south of France. This also applies to plants from South American countries such as Chile and Peru, where many of the most beautiful trees and shrubs come from. The climatic zones explain the reasons why plants from the Southern Hemisphere, for example, are hardy in Normandy and Britain, while many North American species grow out of doors in Germany; and also why the sub-tropical and other tender species introduced during the seventeenth and eighteenth centuries require treatment under glass.

This map of climatic zones shows that countries in quite different parts of the world often have similar climates.

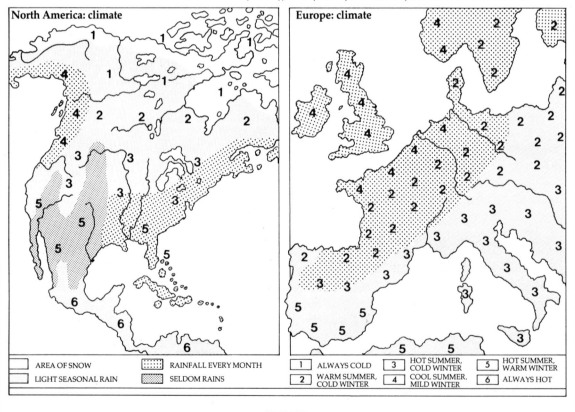

Glasshouses

Originally a glass- or greenhouse was for evergreens, and its purpose, like that of an orangery, was to protect plants grown in pots or tubs over the winter months, so that they might be carried out in summer and placed along the terraces and walks of gardens.

Among the popular evergreens of this period were *Myrtus*, *Arbutus*, Laurel (*Prunus laurocerasus*), Portugal Laurel (*P. lusitanica*) Common Box (*Buxus sempervirens*) and Sweet Bay (*Laurus nobilis*). Sometimes these were trained with round heads and clean stems up to a height of about 2 metres (7 feet), or else clipped as pyramids or cones. Yew (*Taxus*) and hollies (*Ilex*) (often *Ilex aquifolium*, *I. a.* 'Ferox' and different variegated forms) were used in the same way. However, even a glasshouse was not enough to guard against the winter cold, so braziers or stoves were placed inside the buildings; but the introduction of tender exotics called for more subtle methods, and underground heating was installed in houses especially built for the cultivation of particular types of plants.

Glasshouses and orangeries were important to the great seventeenth- and eighteenth-century gardens of Europe, and they were popular in the smaller houses, providing many of the blooms in the flower garden seen from the house.

Flower Gardens

The English flower garden attached to a modest mansion, described by John Rea in *Flora, Ceres and Pomona* (1655), was similar

The frontispiece of 'Hortus Floridus' shows the variety of bulbs grown during the seventeenth century.

in design to that depicted forty years before in *Hortus Floridus* by Crispin de Passe, published in Arnhem in 1614.

According to Rea, a 3-metre (10-foot) wall surrounding the garden was divided into two unequal parts by a lower wall or paling running perpendicular to it. The smaller area, overlooked from the house, gave direct access to the larger fruit garden. Fruit trees, including vines, played an important role in gardens at that time and were often trained against the walls.

The flower garden was composed of narrow borders and small beds, all of the same width. The borders ran along the foot of the walls and the beds were separated by gravelled or sanded paths. In an area of 25 metres square (30 yards square) there might be as many as twenty-three beds and borders, edged with Dwarf Box, painted wooden boards or stones. On the south wall, peaches and nectarines were planted 3.5 metres (12 feet) apart and alternated with Honeysuckle (*Lonicera*), *Clematis* or vines (*Vitis*), and choice shrubs such as the Double Pomegranate (*Punica granatum*) were placed in the corners of the walls. East and west walls were suitable for plum and cherry trees and the north for pears, with tall standard roses planted in between. The plants recommended for this particular border were auriculas (*Primula auricula*), the double red *Primula vulgaris*, hepaticas, the Double Lychnis, Sweet Rocket (*Hesperis matronalis*), wallflowers (*Cheiranthus*), stocks (*Matthiola*) and gilly-flowers (*Dianthus*).

The advice for planting the corner beds in a flower garden was that the best 'Crown Imperial (*Fritillaria imperialis*), lilies, Martagons (*Lilium martagon*) and such tall flowers' should be planted in the centre of the beds with 'great Tufts of peonies (*Paeonia*) and about them several

The Crown Imperial, introduced to England from Turkey.

sorts of *Cyclamen*; the rest with daffodils (*Narcissus*), hyacinths (*Hyacinthus*)', keeping the straight borders for tulips (*Tulipa*) and placing anemones and ranunculuses in separate beds.

Another border ran along the sides of a rose hedge and here the roses were threaded through the lattice, or frame, which served as a support; on the edge of this border mixed crocuses were planted 'for all seasons'. In the summer *Nerium oleander* and Myrtle, taken from the green-house, were placed on either side of the hedge and stands were provided for flowering plants in pots.

Following the spring-flowering bulbs, aquilegias and irises led on to asphodels (*Asphodeline*) and lupins (*Lupinus*), while

13

L. Rosa centifolia Batavica.

L. Rosa versicolor.

The striped 'Rosa Mundi' is a sport from 'R. gallica officinalis'.

gillyflowers (*Dianthus*) and tradescantias carried the season through to the later flowering plants such as *Delphinium*, *Campanula*, and foxgloves (*Digitalis*), and lastly the North American *Aster* (*Aster novi-belgii*) and scarlet *Lobelia* (*Lobelia cardinalis*).

As well as herbaceous plants, it was possible to have roses in bloom from May until August. Starting with *Rosa cinnamomea* (for warm and sheltered situations), there was the Double White (*Rosa alba maxima*) and the sweet-scented pale red Provins rose. Among the pink ones were *R. damascena*, a variegated form known in England as 'York and Lancaster', and another striped variety called *Rosa mundi* which was a sport of *R. gallica officinalis*,

the Apothecary's Rose or Rose of Provins. There were others, too: the Velvet, the Marbled and the Great Red (*R. centifolia*), which were considered suitable for walls, and the double *R. centifolia muscosa*, which was used in a lattice or a hedge. No doubt the Sweet Briar (*R. rubiginosa*) also had its place in the flower garden, but outside it was valued in the wilderness, where fragrant plants were prized.

The Wilderness and Grove
The wilderness was the link between the seventeenth-century formal French and Dutch gardens and the later landscape designs of William Kent and Capability Brown.

A wilderness was either cut out of an

existing wood or else planted with quick growing deciduous trees. Shaped into squares, angles and circles, the wilderness was surrounded by straight walks hemmed in by hedges of Hornbeam (*Carpinus*), Elm (*Ulmus*), Lime (*Tilia*) or evergreens such as Holly (*Ilex*), Yew (*Taxus*) and Bay (*Laurus nobilis*). As tastes changed to labyrinths and meandering paths, some of the hedges were removed to show spring-flowering

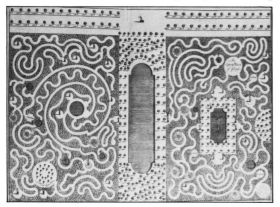

This intricate plan of winding paths is from Batty Langley's 'New Principles of Gardening', 1728.

Primula, Narcissus, the English Bluebell (*Endymion non-scriptus*) and Viola growing naturalistically in the grass. When the concealed angles of the wilderness were opened up, they revealed roses and low-growing shrubs such as daphnes (*D. mezereum*), brooms (*Cytisus*) or hypericums, backed by tall shrubs – for instance, *Syringa, Philadelphus* and *Laburnum*. Woven through these were *Clematis*, Honeysuckle (*Lonicera*) or *Rosa rubiginosa*, plants also used to cover an arbour or a bower.

The garden contained groves as well, bordering shady walks. There were two types of grove: the 'open' and the 'closed'. The first consisted of large trees grown so that the tips of the branches almost touched; they provided shade, but with

sufficient light to allow the grass to grow. A closed grove with tall trees was underplanted with shrubs to give privacy and shelter, or used to disguise an eyesore; sometimes it surrounded an entire garden. Here again, on either side of the gravelled walks, sweet-scented flowers or shrubs would be planted, forming a thicket, or *bosquet* (coppice).

Pleasure Grounds

The pleasure ground included almost all sections of which a garden was composed and each was connected by a well kept walk.

Choice trees and shrubs were scattered on the lawn or grew in large beds or borders of mixed planting (trees and shrubs mingled with herbaceous plants), sometimes sheltered by a grove or hedge. A recommendation for the pleasure grounds was that 'beds of ` bog earth' should be prepared for American plants such as American species of *Magnolia, Rhododendron, Kalmia* and other acid-loving plants from the eastern states. If, however, a garden was designed for botanical interest, their plants were deployed with this in mind and not just for picturesque effect.

Exotics in the European Garden

Seafaring countries with colonial links, such as those of England, France and Holland, were pre-eminent in the introduction of exotic plants. This, combined with the connections which Britain and France had with North America, accounts for their introductions of exotics from the west, while Holland will always be renowned for importing African species via the Cape of Good Hope. Otherwise, most European countries were the indirect recipients of exotic plants.

In Spain, for instance, the gardens of grandees were formal in design and did not call for exotics until the Botanic Garden in Madrid was founded in 1755. In Lombardy the introduction of foreign trees and shrubs took place in about 1770, when the first garden in the English manner was planted at Cremona. Soon afterwards two Dutchmen living in Italy introduced a great number and variety of hardy plants from Holland.

Meanwhile, in America one of the most beautiful examples of a landscaped garden had almost reached maturity. This was Middleton Place, near Charleston in South Carolina, which was laid out in 1741. It was here that the camellias, first introduced to North America by André Michaux, were planted in 1783.

For a long time North America was one of the main areas from which European gardens drew their hardy plants. Among the first North American hardies to grow in Europe were *Thuja occidentalis* and *Yucca gloriosa*, which were recorded as early as 1596, and by the first half of the seventeenth century, the Swamp or Bald Cypress (*Taxodium distichum*) and Tulip Tree (*Liriodendron tulipifera*) were well established while *Robinia pseudacacia* grew in Le Jardin des Plantes. Later, the Bishop of London, who was responsible for the Anglican Church abroad, received plants and seeds from one of his ministers in Virginia, and before the century was out *Magnolia virginiana*, *Liquidambar styraciflua* and *Oxydendrum arboreum* were growing in the Bishop's London garden. During the next century, a great number of North American species were introduced and spread through the gardens of Europe by a system of exchange.

In England, Peter Collinson, a London merchant, established a correspondence

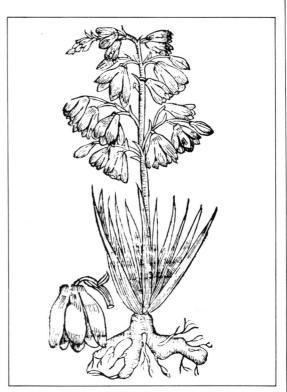

Yucca gloriosa and other hardy plants were introduced to Europe from America as early as 1596.

with John Bartram of Philadelphia in 1734, and through him imported North American plants and seeds on behalf of friends and subscribers in the British Isles. Soon he was exchanging seeds with botanists abroad. His correspondents included the famous botanist Linnaeus, and Doctors Gronovius of Amsterdam and Amman of Russia and, far away in China, a French missionary, Père d'Incarville.

At the same time, the French maintained their interest in North American trees through André Michaux, who collected and sent home many species of American oaks (*Quercus*) and other plants. By 1789, the year of the French Revolution, new species were available from China and Japan. But meanwhile, in England, fashions had changed.

The English Garden

In the early eighteenth century, the English still modelled their gardens on those of the French and Dutch. But as English taste swung towards a more natural style of planting, the park became the important part of the prospect from the house. Long avenues of trees were broken up and native trees were grouped in squares or clumps. By degrees, the elaborate formal gardens, hitherto arranged around the house, were removed and the kitchen garden was relegated to some distant place. By the middle of the century, immense plantations of native trees spread across the countryside and, thanks to the ha-ha, there was an uninterrupted view of the whole park from the house. In the process of landscaping, hills were removed or valleys made; streams were diverted to form lakes and serpentine lines wound through the woods, wilderness and groves. This new type of gardening was later adopted in Europe, where it became fashionable to plant an English garden.

The transition from formal to informal took place during the first half of the eighteenth century in England, and from about the third decade botanical collections were assembled in modest gardens round London and elsewhere; these were filled with North American and Chinese plants, all of which were arranged according to a natural system in regular rows, as in botanic gardens, or grouped together ornamentally, and surrounded by gravelled

'Le jardin Anglais' became a style of garden adapted throughout Europe in the eighteenth century.

paths and sheltered by dense plantations of hardy evergreen trees and shrubs.

As more plants were introduced from both the East and West, further developments in planning English gardens were required. Now American trees and shrubs such as North American oaks (*Quercus*), maples (*Acer*), *Catalpa*, walnuts (*Juglans*), aralias, and species of *Cornus* and *Rhus* were planted to form groves, and American magnolias, kalmias, rhododendrons and other peat-loving plants were assembled in beds and borders, which were referred to as American gardens, grounds or groves. Chinese species were arranged together to form Chinese gardens. The same principle of planting was adopted in Europe, where, in some areas, it was necessary to exercise more care in selecting hardy plants.

One of the first examples of an English garden in Germany was at the Garten der Schwobber in Westphalia, which was laid out in about 1750, with clumps of trees, winding walks and a notable collection of rare plants. There are also records of similar gardens of about the same date in Hanover and later, Field Marshal Lacy employed an Englishman to plan his garden in the new style near Vienna. In France in about 1763, part of the old garden at Versailles was removed and replaced by a garden *à l'Anglais*. The best French examples surviving are at Ermenonville and Bagatelle.

When the Empress Joséphine created a garden at Malmaison with the aid of French and English gardeners, she adopted a new style of garden design in order to display roses and other plants. The Empress obtained some of the plants for her botanical collection from English nurserymen, in spite of Franco-British wars.

In Paris, another much smaller garden – only two acres in extent – was modelled on the English garden. Its owner, Monsieur Boursault, filled it with rare species which, although known in Britain for several years, were found nowhere else in France. In spite of the limited space, the garden included most of the exotics already introduced plus an impressive collection of additional plants. They included camellias and 'numerous rhododendrons and azaleas', as well as two species of *Magnolia* and other Chinese and Japanese plants such as *Michelia*, *Photinia*, *Koelreuteria*, *Nandina* and *Cunninghamia*; there was also an unidentified species of Bamboo (*Arundinaria*), and 'a collection of standard roses' which was 'remarkably complete'. One of Boursault's contemporaries considered that, outside Le Jardin des Plantes, this was the best collection of plants in France.

The plan of M. Boursault's garden in Paris.

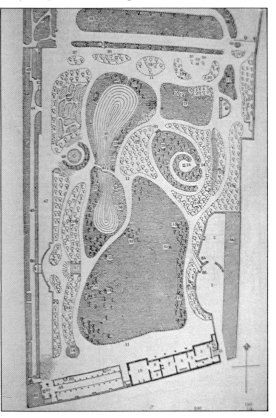

Rose Gardens

Rose gardens or roseries are of relatively recent date, but during the first half of the nineteenth century there were examples in Denmark and the Netherlands. Although roses at this date were cultivated under glass in Munich and Berlin they could be seen in Baden in almost every garden out of doors. The Italians in particular excelled in the cultivation of the rose.

The first hybrid roses raised in America were of a cross between *Rosa chinensis* and *R. moschata* by John Champneys of Charleston who, in 1811, selected a seedling of this cross which he gave to a neighbouring nurseryman of French descent called Philip Noisette, whose name became associated with roses of this type.

However, in Paris, M. Boursault's garden conformed to nineteenth-century ideas. He grouped his standard roses as single specimens on a lawn, or in the midst of flower beds, or as borders along a walk. At the Grand Trianon at Versailles, they were massed like a plantation of trees and shrubs, with more vigorous varieties trained up a framework of poles to form a cone. A popular method was to lay them out in a geometrical design with paths and beds edged with clipped dwarf box.

Baskets of roses were another example of nineteenth-century taste: these were oval beds surrounded with box edging or 'baskets' of wickerwork or wire, about 20.5 cm

The Rosary at Ashridge from Repton's 'Fragments on the Theory and Practice of Landscape Gardening', 1816.

A Victorian Rose Garden

To make a Victorian-style rose garden choose a geometrical design, keeping the shapes simple and allowing ample width on your beds and borders; nineteenth-century roses are generally larger growing than modern Hybrid Teas, often attaining a height and spread of about 1.5m (5ft). Use ironwork to give your plan three-dimensional form and to provide a framework for the roses, as in the recreated Victorian rose garden at Warwick Castle in Warwickshire (see plan). Lengths of mild steel can easily be bent to the shape required by a metal worker, and must then be galvanized and painted (to protect them from rust) and set in concrete for stability.

The roses available to Victorian gardeners are still among the most glorious of all, with their soft colours, full-petalled forms and exquisite fragrance. At the beginning of the nineteenth century the most popular roses were the Gallica, Centifolia and Moss roses, which were all 'summer flowering' – that is, they had one brief, splendid period of bloom and then scarcely another flower for the rest of the summer. However, after the introduction of the China rose in the middle of the century, rose breeders produced many new hybrid varieties with a longer flowering season, such as the Bourbons and the Hybrid Perpetuals. Include these in your selection of roses to ensure flowers throughout the summer. Many commercial rose growers are proud of their collections of 'old roses'; study their catalogues, and if possible, visit their nurseries during the rose season before making your choice.

To finish the garden, try to find cast-iron seats in Victorian designs, like the fern pattern seats used in the rose garden shown. To be truly authentic paint them chocolate brown, just as they were originally offered for sale in the Coalbrookdale catalogue of the period.

The Victorian rose garden at Warwick Castle, Warwickshire (shown below), is in the process of re-creation under the guidance of Paul Edwards, based on the original plan of 1864 by Robert Marnock.

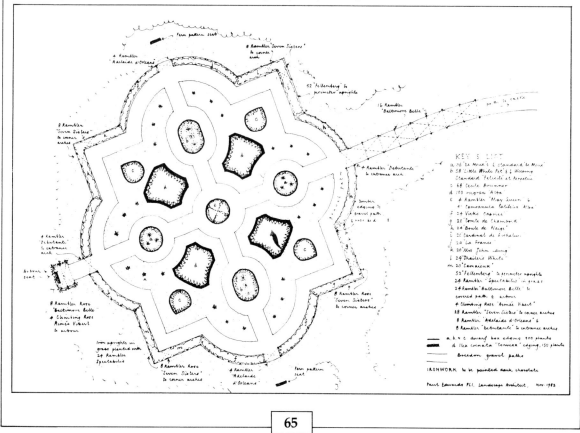

(1 foot) high, bordered by a narrow strip of lawn or gravelled paths; within the 'basket' the ground was raised into a mound and then planted with rose bushes, the shoots of which were pegged down so that the tips took root. After a year or two, when in bloom, only the flowers along the stem were visible, resembling a basket of flowers.

Usually rose beds consisted of a single variety, but if mixed, care was taken to ensure that the selected plants were of similar habit, flower and leaf and that the colours were an obvious contrast. Sometimes they were filled with a single species such as the Scotch (*R. pimpinellifolia* or *spinosissima*), Chinese (hybrids of *R. chinensis*) or *R. virginiana* grown in separate beds, and sometimes climbing roses were encouraged to grow up artificial rockwork in the centre of the beds, or else standard roses were planted as a group and the whole surrounded by a trellis of roses. Alternatively, roses were trained up poles and then strung as swags.

Nineteenth-century Flower Gardens

The earlier parterre was later incorporated into nineteenth-century gardens; its intricate patterns allowed for different varieties of flowers to be grown, depended on contrasting colours and seasons and was suited to massed planting. In France and Germany, the flower beds were usually surrounded by gravelled paths, but in England they tended to be cut out of well-trimmed lawns. One complicated English garden consisted of 120 different beds designed for spring-, summer- and autumn-flowering plants; beds were reserved for anemones, crocuses, hyacinths, *Narcissi*, violas and oenotheras, with snowdrops (*Galanthus*) planted round the margins of beds of tulips or ranunculuses.

For summer and autumn, standard roses were underplanted with *Verbena* and *Lobelia*. Mixed calceolarias grew in one bed and heliotropes (*Heliotropium*) and pelargoniums in another. Different species of *Fuchsia* were planted together, as were sages; *Lobelia* was mixed with *Campanula*, while other beds were set aside for dahlias. (On the other hand a French parterre, with scrolls or small beds edged with dwarf box, was filled with different coloured sands and these looked well throughout the year.)

Although the 'English' garden was now popular in Germany, for formal gardens the Dutch and Germans still clung to French ideas instead of the English style of bedding out. In England, massed planting was sometimes used with flowers of one kind and colour, such as scarlet geraniums, or one large bed was divided to display particular types of plants – bulbs, for instance, or a mixture of bulbs and annuals, or annuals on their own – or there might be a 'changeable' Chinese garden. In the latter, plants in flower were arranged in their pots, while others were kept in nursery ground to replace them when required, thus ensuring that the whole effect could be changed or renewed within a matter of hours.

Arboretums and Pinetums

Explorations in the west of North America in 1804 opened up a new area for botanists. One of them, David Douglas, a Scot, was sent to America in search of plants by the Horticultural Society of London. Between 1823 and 1834 he travelled in the eastern and western states and in Canada, sending back an immense and varied collection of trees and shrubs, among other plants. These, together with Mexican and Himalayan species, which were introduced to Europe during the nineteenth century,

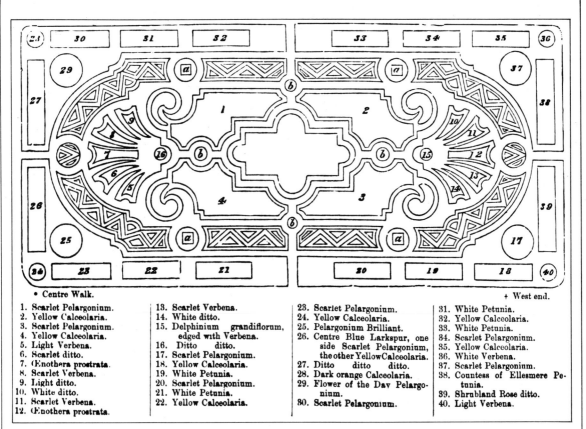

• Centre Walk.		+ West end.

1. Scarlet Pelargonium.
2. Yellow Calceolaria.
3. Scarlet Pelargonium.
4. Yellow Calceolaria.
5. Light Verbena.
6. Scarlet ditto.
7. Œnothera prostrata.
8. Scarlet Verbena.
9. Light ditto.
10. White ditto.
11. Scarlet Verbena.
12. Œnothera prostrata.

13. Scarlet Verbena.
14. White ditto.
15. Delphinium grandiflorum, edged with Verbena.
16. Ditto ditto.
17. Scarlet Pelargonium.
18. Yellow Calceolaria.
19. White Petunia.
20. Scarlet Pelargonium.
21. White Petunia.
22. Yellow Calceolaria.

23. Scarlet Pelargonium.
24. Yellow Calceolaria.
25. Pelargonium Brilliant.
26. Centre Blue Larkspur, one side Scarlet Pelargonium, the other Yellow Calceolaria.
27. Ditto ditto ditto.
28. Dark orange Calceolaria.
29. Flower of the Day Pelargonium.
30. Scarlet Pelargonium.

31. White Petunia.
32. Yellow Calceolaria.
33. White Petunia.
34. Scarlet Pelargonium.
35. Yellow Calceolaria.
36. White Verbena.
37. Scarlet Pelargonium.
38. Countess of Ellesmere Petunia.
39. Shrubland Rose ditto.
40. Light Verbena.

William Nesfield's plan for a Victorian garden is planted with brilliant annuals.

North American conifers in the dell at Bodnant.

were incorporated into the pleasure ground, or arboretums were created especially for trees.

The boundaries of pleasure grounds had now been reached and exotic trees were grouped in the park, or planted as single specimens on the edges of the woods or drives, or on the main avenue leading to the house. They were arranged according to their botanical classification, with each genus being planted separately in the arboretum, or they were placed in geographical order, the trees of the Americas, China, Australasia and Japan being grown in distinct groups, according to their countries of origin. Most pleasure grounds included a pinetum, where conifers of every sort were grown.

Many conifers are native to Europe and the Mediterranean region, and various North American species had been grown in Europe for two or three hundred years. Previously trees such as the Aleppo or Weymouth Pines (*Pinus halepensis* and *P. strobus*) had been dispersed among the other plants, but now they were confined to pinetums, where the trees were grouped in the same way as those in arboretums. If they were treated according to their botanical classification, then cypresses, junipers, pines or Spruce were placed in separate groups. Alternatively, if they were geographically arranged, then the trees of each country were placed separately. However, certain species of magnificent habit, such as *Cedrus libani*, were isolated in the park or on lawns near the house. *Taxodium distichum*, a native of south-east American swamps, was planted by a lake or stream, but dwarf conifers, unable to compete with trees, were often used to create a decorative feature by a rock or in rock gardens.

Rock Gardens

Rock work had long been used in gardens for picturesque effect; rock gardens were constructed from the middle of the nineteenth century, to imitate the natural habitat of alpine plants. An exemplary example of picturesque rockwork was to be found in 1828 at a villa garden near Paris, where the house overlooked a heap of boulders with a fountain in its centre. Surviving Irish examples, made twenty or thirty years later, show that, by then, rockeries were carefully planned and built with rustic arches, narrow walks and pools surrounded by rough stones. These pools were supplied by naturally running, or artificially supplied, piped water and shaded by tall trees. Growing among the

'A Parisian rock garden with fountain' from J. C. Loudon's 'Encyclopaedia of Gardening', 1850.

rocks were various ferns, nearby perhaps a specimen of Bamboo (*Arundinaria*) and the Chusan and Cabbage Palms (*Chamaerops* and *Cordyline*), and there were foliage plants, such as hostas from Japan, which created a cool green atmosphere.

In contrast, the rock gardens designed for alpine plants required an open situation with a proper depth of soil. If necessary, imported boulders were used as substitutes for local rock. Unless built on sloping ground, they were constructed so that from ground level they rose to 3 to 3.5 metres (10 to 12 feet) or more, from which it was possible to survey the garden and, close by, large boulders were placed in small beds in the grass beside a conifer.

Most rock gardens contained a few of the

Water Gardens

Eighteenth-century lakes, their banks embellished by temples and grottoes, can be seen in England at Stourhead, in France at Ermenonville and at Wurlite in Germany. At the time they were designed, the planting was restrained, with use being made of *Liriodendron tulipifera* and *Taxodium distichum*. Now lakes are still surrounded by such trees, but with the addition of nyssas, liquidambars and *Rhododendron* (*R. ponticum*), usually planted in the last century. However, since then lakes and streams have lent themselves to a more elaborate type of planting.

The appearance of a water garden, highlighted by bridges and bronze lanterns, was often Japanese. But while *Acer palmatum* in its different forms is entirely Japanese, in fact indispensable plants such as *Gunnera manicata*, *Osmunda* and the yellow-flowered Bog Arum (*Lysichitum*), with their magnificent foliage, come from other parts of the world.

Weeping trees, the Weeping Willow (*Salix babylonica*), for instance, or *Pyrus salicifolia* 'Pendula', look beautiful by water, as do those with outstanding cream or whitish stems such as Birch (*Betula*) or, in winter, the red-stemmed Alder, *Alnus incana* 'Aurea'. Herbaceous plants – hostas, rodgersias, irises, day lilies (*Hemerocallis*) and astilbes – grew in narrow borders around a pond, while the Candelabra Primula, *P. japonica*, introduced in 1871, was ideal in slanting shade.

Bamboos, particularly *Arundinaria anceps*, belong to this lakeside area and were used as a background or a screen. Other species, especially the forms with variegated leaves, made attractive clumps, and some of the grasses were used in the same way – a species of *Miscanthus*, for example, which grows up to a height of

Irises, Ferns and Day Lilies go to make a varied waterside tableau at Dunmore Manor, near Hereford.

dwarf conifers which were available at the time and one or two forms of *Acer palmatum* 'Dissectum', plus every imaginable type of alpine plant, ranging from species of dwarf bulbs to pinks (*Dianthus*) and *Phlox*. There were mats of purple Thyme (*Thymus*), bright blue gentians, *Lithospermum diffusum* and Cranesbill (*Geranium*); and saxifrages and sedums were tucked in between the rocks. On the shaded side of the rock garden were the low European alpine rhododendrons, *R. hirsutum* and *R. ferrugineum*, with other plants such as heaths and heathers and species of *Vaccinium* or *Gaultheria*; while Mediterranean rock-roses (*Cistus*) and brooms (*Genista* and *Cytisus*) were encouraged to sprawl among the rocks.

about 2 metres (7 feet) and has arched leaves with cream or golden stripes.

In the last quarter of the nineteenth century in England, a fashion for wild gardening set in.

Wild Gardens

Although the planting round a water garden was contrived with care, it was in keeping with a new fashion which started in England during the last quarter of the nineteenth century, when William Robinson began to plant 'wild' gardens. In this way he rebelled against the re-appearance of parterres, bedding out and topiary in English gardens, as his eighteenth-century forbears had turned against the formal gardens based on French and Dutch design. From that period – the early eighteenth century – in England, there was an emphasis on the introduction of new species and a style of 'natural' planting, which today is still the hallmark of the English garden.

The purpose of 'Robinsonian', or wild, gardens was to establish exotics where they would care for themselves in the pleasure grounds or in surrounding fields and meadows. This style was adopted in the British Isles where it became widespread, but although it did not spread in Europe, later it was copied in America. Not only exotics but native species were also encouraged in the woods by the wide distribution of snowdrops (*Galanthus*), daffodils, the English Bluebell (*Endymion nonscriptus*) and Wood Anemone (*Anemone nemorosa*). In addition forms of the blue *A. nemorosa* and Winter Aconite (*Eranthis hiemalis*) and other species were planted under individual trees. A typical example of such planting can be seen at Winterthur in Delaware. Ferns and kingcups were established by brooks, and periwinkles (*Vinca*) and cyclamens in the woods; Robinson planted daffodils in the fields and trained *Wisteria* up trees. In the process, he recommended plants such as *Convolvulus*, which soon got out of hand; and it was quickly realized that other species, North American *Aster* and *Solidago*, for example, looked better in herbaceous borders than in grass.

Herbaceous and Flower Borders

The era of herbaceous borders was at its peak in England during the first part of the twentieth century and occasionally the idea was copied on the continent. Gertrude Jekyll, who was one of England's greatest advocates of this type of planting, designed borders for the gardens of Le Bois des Moutiers in Normandy, and for two gardens in America – at Perintown in Ohio and the Old Glebe House in Connecticut – but on the whole, for climatic reasons, they were especially associated with gardens in the British Isles, their popularity lasting until the outbreak of the Second World War.

Herbaceous borders were found either in or outside walled gardens, near the house, or somewhere in the pleasure grounds, where they were sheltered by evergreen hedges up to a height of about 2 metres (7 feet).

An old wall of stone or brick was an excellent backdrop and provided a mellow-coloured support for roses and evergreens, while no hedge surpassed that of Yew (*Taxus*) as a background for herbaceous or perennial plants, although *Ilex aquifolium* or *Chamaecyparis lawsoniana* were often used instead.

Gertrude Jekyll advised that a space of 1 metre (3¼ feet) should be left between the wall and the back of the border to allow room to care for the plants in the border

Colourful herbaceous borders at Bramdean lead out into the rolling green of the English countryside.

and those growing on the wall – a practical point which applied equally well to the maintenance of hedges. She also recommended 4 metres (14 feet) as a good width for borders, and 2 metres (7 feet) for paths.

Against the walls in mild climates one might expect to find evergreen species of *Myrtus, Feijoa, Ceanothus, Carpenteria* or *Crinodendron* interplanted with some of the roses which required support, such as *Rosa* 'Fantin Latour' or 'Souvenir de la Malmaison'. This was the place for half-hardy species of *Abutilon*, Australian *Leptospermum*, clematises or vines (*Vitis*). In colder areas, evergreen shrubs might include *Viburnum tinus*, some of the variegated hollies (*Ilex*), *Camellia, Magnolia* or *Garrya elliptica* and between these other varieties of *Clematis, Chaenomeles*, Jasmine (*Jasmi-*

num) or Honeysuckle (*Lonicera*). This, too, was a place for climbing roses.

Pairs of plants were sometimes used to emphasize a point. For instance, if borders were broken by a path and arch leading to some other part of the garden, shrubs of a pleasing habit and colour, *Choisya ternata* or Irish Yew (*Taxus fastigiata*), were placed on either side of the path or at the corners of small borders edged with Box (*Buxus*), and sometimes there were small specimens of this shrub clipped in the shape of pyramids or globes. *Yucca* underplanted with *Bergenia* made another focal point.

Some borders were confined to a particular type of plant or colour. Silver borders consisted of Jerusalem Sage (*Phlomis*) and shrubby *Senecio* in addition to sub-shrubs such as *Artemisia, Santolina* or *Sene-*

cio cineraria. At the back of the border were tall plants, Scotch Thistle (*Onopordon*), for instance, and silvery leaved *Verbascum*. In the centre were lower plants, *Romneya* and *Gypsophila*, with *Stachys* or carnations (*Dianthus*) at the front.

Blue borders contained delphiniums and lupins and the low sub-shrubs *Perovskia* or *Caryopteris*, with irises, blue cranesbills and *Nepeta*; and for summer and autumn there were spectacular borders to display Michaelmas daisies (*Aster*) or dahlias. But borders of mixed flowers were planned like jigsaw puzzles with plants of one kind interlocked in blocks with others of different shapes and sizes. One or two shrubs, hydrangeas or *Euphorbia wulfenii*, were included in such borders. Perennial plants were mixed with annuals: tall sun flowers (*Helianthus*) and hollyhocks (*Althea rosea*) at the back; *Iberis*, Sage and marigolds (*Tagetes*) in front and, in between, *Campanula* and *Achillea*. All were carefully graded in height from front to rear, and in colour, from one end of the border to the other; the colours ranging, for example, from white to blue, yellow, orange and red and, in the same order, back to white.

Tubs and pots were used for growing *Agapanthus*, *Fuchsia*, geraniums or *Hydrangea* and these were placed by gates or steps. One particularly attractive plant for this purpose was *Rhododendron* 'Lady Alice Fitzwilliam', which in mild areas could be grown in a sheltered corner in the woods.

Rhododendron Gardens

The introduction to Europe of Chinese and Himalayan species of rhododendron before and after the First World War required more space in the garden. But of course the problem of space only arose in areas within the oceanic zones.

At Le Bois des Moutiers in Normandy, there is a bank of *Rhododendron* × 'Halopeanum' (*R. griffithianum* × *R. maximum*) which was planted at the beginning of the century, and there are specimens of old hardy hybrids as well as species such as *R. griffithianum* and *R. makinoi*; but nowhere, perhaps, are rhododendrons seen so well as in regions of high rainfall in the British Isles.

It was fortuitous that in England in areas of acid soil the only vacant ground sur-

A Colour Border

The herbaceous border reached its peak of popularity in the early years of this century. To recreate one of a specific colour in your garden first make a careful planting plan, taking local climatic and soil conditions into consideration. Plan well in advance, drawing up your plant list carefully and finding reliable suppliers. If necessary, order from specialist growers.

As a general rule herbaceous perennials are the main constituent of the border, and, as these plants enjoy the sun, a south facing site backed by a wall is ideal. The border should be a minimum width of 2.5 metres (8 feet) and prepared by double digging with plenty of humus-making material – such as manure or garden compost – the autumn before planting. It is important that the soil should be rich enough to sustain dense planting and healthy growth: a sparse border is a depressing sight.

The name 'white border' or 'red border' would seem to indicate exclusivity, but for maximum effect this is not strictly so. A white border is accentuated by the inclusion of 'silver' plants and a scattering of yellow flowers, a red border made more sumptuous and dramatic by the use of bronze or purple foliage plants. On this page are two suggested planting plans that will enable you to enjoy a white and a red border in your garden. Both plans assume the existence of a fence or a wall at the back. Check that conditions in your area are suitable for the plants, and if necessary find alternatives – ask your supplier for advice.

rounding private gardens were often woods of native Oak (*Quercus*), some of which were already full of *Rhododendron ponticum*. By making use of the shelter these supplied, clearing the undergrowth and lopping trees, room was found for all the new species of rhododendron. The good drainage and dappled shade, and an accumulation of leaf mould, provided the perfect conditions for these new plants.

Almost all rhododendron species and many hybrids are extremely beautiful, but if the constitution of a species is in doubt then a hybrid makes a useful substitute. For instance, R. × Hawk v. 'Crest' is an admirable alternative for species such as *R. campylocarpum* or *R. wardii* which, though relatively hardy, are of a more delicate habit and constitution. No plants illustrate the value of hybrids more effectively than the first cross made in 1831 between *R. catawbiense × ponticum* and the red form of the Himalayan *R. arboreum*, a cross which produced *R.* Altaclerense. Although few

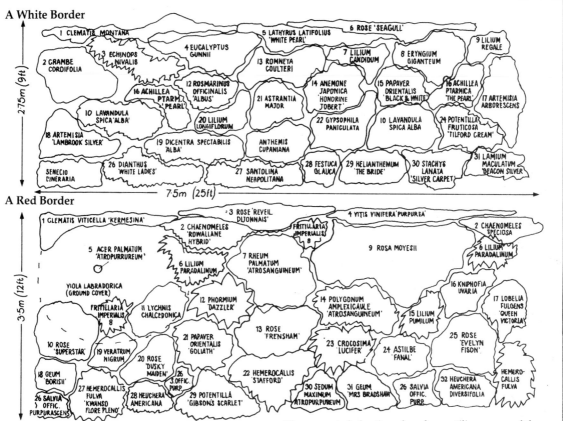

A White Border

2·75m (9ft)

7·5m (25ft)

A Red Border

3·5m (12ft)

A suggested planting plan for a white border, which includes many silver-leaved plants and contrasting foliage shapes. The back wall is festooned with quick growing clematises and a sweet-scented rambling rose. During the spring plant plenty of snowdrops and narcissi, and the graceful tulip 'White Triumphator'.

The suggested planting plan above utilizes many of the plants in the famous red borders at Hidcote Manor, Glos. The plants selected for this border are principally hardy perennials, but trees, shrubs and Floribunda roses are included to give it a permanent framework. For spring display plant narcissi, the brilliant red species tulips and groups of exotic-looking Crown Imperials.

Naturalized Cyclamen neapolitanum, in the partial shade of this woodland garden.

A mixed planting of rhododendrons and azaleas thrive in the dappled shade of woodland.

PLANTS AND PLANTING

*Herbaceous borders
became popular in
England and America
at the beginning of the
twentieth century.
They were often
confined to a
particular type of
plant or colour. Here
white Dianthus and
Stachys lanata
border the paths to
create this 'white'
garden at Sissinghurst.*

A purple border, seen here at Sissinghurst. For specific planting plans and advice see pages 72 and 73.

people ventured to plant *R. arboreum* along the main drive leading to the house, they sometimes planted avenues of *R. 'Altaclerense'*, which can be seen in full vigour to this day. This remarkable red rhododendron was used extensively from an early date and any of the 'hardy hybrids', as they are called, with a background such as these, were often planted in the open and were even used as screens.

By the beginning of the present century, further hybrids were raised by crossing the Chinese *R. fortunei* with *R. griffithianum* (the latter grows at a height of 2,743 metres [9,000 feet] in Bhutan), from which arose varieties of *R.* × *Loderi*, which are distinguished by their immense trusses of pink or white sweet-scented flowers. Later innumerable hybrid rhododendrons were raised in the period between the two world wars.

Nurserymen in Belgium, Holland and Great Britain developed the groups of azalea (these are classified as *Rhododendrons*) known as Occidentale, Ghent, Mollis, Knap Hill and so on, and the evergreen azaleas developed in Japan, Europe and America found a place in the woods under a light canopy of shade. These, with American species such as *R. arborescens* or *R. viscosum*, were either planted in beds, or mixed in borders in the shrubbery. Finally a note should be made of those known in England as 'Wilson's Fifty' – the azaleas introduced to America by an Englishman and plant collector, E. H. Wilson, who became director of the Arnold Arboretum at Boston in the United States of America.

Peat Gardens

The peat garden evolved from the 'beds of bog earth' prepared for American plants imported in the eighteenth century. As many of these were members of the Ericaceous family, such as *Erica*, *Rhododendrons*, *Vaccinium* or *Gaultheria*, they were associated with other introductions which enjoyed the same conditions but came from other parts of the world.

A peat garden was composed of beds built up with peat blocks, and loam mixed liberally with peat, in a position which received slanting shade. This was the place for Himalayan Blue Poppy (*Meconopsis*), *Primula* and lilies, and the dwarf species of rhododendrons with diminutive grey-blue leaves. Here, North American *Uvularia* flowered with *Trillium*, or gentians were mixed with *Polygonum* and North American Dog's Tooth Violets (*Erythronium*), and those from Europe and Japan grew side by side. Some of New Zealand's choice *Celmisia* and other Australasian plants thrive in the peat garden.

Making Room for More Exotics

Australasian plants, introduced to Europe at the end of the eighteenth century, were generally grown under glass. Although most are unsuited to a continental climate, many are hardy in the Riviera region or in the British Isles.

No particular part of a garden was set aside for exotics from the Southern Hemisphere, and they were scattered through the pleasure grounds. *Eucryphia* from South America and Australia and the Chilean Fire Bush (*Embothrium*) were grown in the shaded side of shrubberies, while New Zealand and Australian *Senecio* and *Olearia* thrive in the sun. The different species of Southern Beech (*Nothofagus*) from all these countries were planted in the woods. By this time only botanic gardens or the great private botanical collections could cope with the influx of so many plants, and individual gardeners began to concentrate

These illustrations from 'Hortus Floridus' by Crispin de Passe (1614) show some of the most sought-after garden plants of the early seventeenth century, many of which remain just as popular today. Sunflowers (Helianthus annuus) and the 'Marvel of Peru' (Mirabilis jalapa) were brought back to Europe by the returning Spanish conquistadores. Iris susiana, hyacinths and clove-scented carnations came from the Moslem gardens of Turkey, and species of Anemone, Cyclamen, Narcissi and Helleborus were among the indigenous wild plants of Europe.

Sunflower (Helianthus)

Iris

Mirabilis

Hyacinth (Hyacinthus)

Carnation (Dianthus)

Cyclamen

Narcissus

Hellebore (Helleborus)

on some particular part of the garden or to specialize in certain types of plant.

The first of the Japanese Cherries of garden origin (*Prunus serrulata*) was introduced to England in about 1880; this was 'Fugenzo'. The variety 'Kanzan' was imported many years later. Japanese cherries were widely planted in private and in public parks. Between 1913 and 1932 there was another new development: some of the greatest botanical collecting journeys were made in the countries which stretched from northern Burma to Tibet. By this time, the horticultural scene was set in Europe and America for the many new species and varieties available. But lack of space became a problem, and gardeners now began to specialize in particular types of plants or gardens.

Twentieth-century Rose Gardens

By 1920 some gardeners deplored the fact that roses were usually grown on their own; they preferred to include them in a

The delicate reflexed petals of Erythronium 'White Beauty' contrast well with their mottled dark foliage.

flower garden, grouped in beds.

At this time, Monthly and Tea roses were fashionable and once again climbing roses, such as the Dundee Rambler, were used to cover shelters, a trellis, or a fence, while others were trained over a pergola, or up a tree. If the garden was walled, some of the newer climbing roses, 'Lady Hillingdon', for instance, or 'Ophelia', 'Madame Butterfly' or 'Etoile de Hollande' were mixed on the walls, with other climbing plants such as *Actinidia*, *Trachelospermum* or *Schizophragma*.

In the beds, the roses, instead of being mulched in the summer, were underplanted with some surface-rooting plants: *Myosotis*, *Aubrieta*, *Viola* or Mignonette (*Reseda*).

Standard roses were also a feature of the period. These were grafted on stems of 1.2 to 1.5 metres (4 to 5 feet) and trained on a mushroom-shaped iron frame, as were American rambling roses such as 'American Pillar' or 'Dorothy Perkins'.

Gardens in America

No country has been more successful in re-creating period gardens than North America. Williamsburg in Virginia is an example of a small late seventeenth-century English country town which has been reconstructed in the present century. Here as much attention has been paid to the re-creation of the gardens as to the buildings in the town. The designs used were similar to those found in small English country towns of the same date, and the only flowers allowed were those known to have been grown at that time. In the same way, street planting was carefully planned; the Paper Mulberry (*Broussonetia papyrifera*), Crape Myrtle (*Lagerstroemia indica*)

The nineteenth-century Roseraie de l'Haÿ displays a profusion of pillar, standard and bedding roses.

and Osage Orange (*Maclura aurantiaca*) were all known in seventeenth-century Virginia; and these may be seen in Williamsburg's gardens or the streets.

The garden at Middleton Place, near Charleston (mentioned earlier), was developed by Henry Middleton, Governor of South Carolina, in the early eighteenth century. Governors of colonies took as keen an interest in introducing useful vegetables and fruit as they did in agricultural crops, and it was but a step from this to ornamental plants. Soon, exotic species were crossing the Atlantic from west to east as well as vice versa.

After the Revolution in America, Thomas Jefferson continued in the same mould as the former governors, sending seeds to Europe and introducing seed himself. Before becoming President he was America's Ambassador in France, from whence he travelled to Holland and England, where he became enamoured of the English style of landscape garden. Eventually he laid out his garden at Monticello in Virginia on these lines.

However, it was in 1873, when Dr Charles Sargent became director of the newly established Arnold Arboretum, at Boston, Massachusetts, that a new era in America's introduction of hardy plants began.

Sargent's objective was to introduce any plant which might prove hardy in New England. Between 1892 and 1906 he travelled in Japan and South America; and between 1907 and 1922, E. H. Wilson, on behalf of the Arnold Arboretum, collected in Japan, Taiwan and Korea. Wilson brought back 1,200 species of trees and shrubs to the benefit of gardens in Europe as well as in America.

Planting summary

Below are just some of the plants grown in the gardens described in the preceding chapter. They should all be available from nurseries or specialist growers, but ask your supplier whether the soil and climate in your area will allow the plants to thrive.

The symbols alongside some of the plants represent the following:

* An evergreen plant

† Too tender for exposed positions in all but the mildest areas, but most hardy on walls or where protected by woodland.

‡ Requires lime-free soil or neutral soil; will not tolerate alkaline or chalky conditions.

Evergreens and Glasshouses
*Arbutus unedo
*Buxus sempervirens
*Myrtus communis
†*Nerium oleander

Flower Gardens
Anemone coronaria
Aquilegia canadensis
Asphodeline lutea
Campanula latifolia
Cheiranthus cheiri
*Clematis cirrhosa
Crocus aureus
Cyclamen europaeum
Dianthus barbatus
Dianthus caryophyllus
Delphinium elatum
Digitalis grandiflora
Fritillaria imperialis
Hepatica triloba
Hesperis matronalis
Hyacinthus romanus
Iris florentina
*Iris foetidissima
Iris germanica
Iris pseudacorus
Lonicera periclymenum
Lobelia cardinalis
Lupinus perennis
Lychnis chalcedonica
Matthiola incana
Narcissus poeticus
Narcissus
 pseudonarcissus
Narcissus tazetta
Paeonia officinalis
Primula auricula
Pulsatilla vulgaris
Ranunculus aconitifolius
Tradescantia virginiana
Tulipa suaveolens
Vitis vinifera

The Wilderness
(before 1700)
*Clematis cirrhosa
Cytisus scoparius
*Hypericum calycinum
Laburnum alpinum
Philadelphus coronarius

*Viola odorata
Viola tricolor

The Grove
(before 1700)
Acer negundo
Acer rubrum
Carpinus betulus
Fraxinus ornus
Juglans nigra
‡*Kalmia latifolia
*Quercus coccifera
Rhus typhina
Tilia × europaea
Ulmus glabra
*Viburnum tinus

Trees and Shrubs for Borders in the Pleasure Grounds
Ailanthus altissima
Amelanchier canadensis
Aralia spinosa
Catalpa bignonioides
†*Cistus ladanifer
*Cistus populifolius
Cornus florida
Crataegus crus-galli
Diospyros virginica
Genista hispanica
Gleditsia triacanthos
Halesia carolina
Hippophaë rhamnoides
*†Magnolia grandiflora
*Phlomis fruticosa
Populus balsamifera
‡*Rhododendron
 maximum
‡*Rhododendron
 ponticum
†*Rosmarinus officinalis
Salix babylonica
Sambucus racemosa
Sorbus aucuparia
Sorbus aria
Syringa persica

The English Garden
(M. Boursault's garden)
†*Arundinaria falconeri
‡*Camellia japonica
 'Donckelarii'

*Cunninghamia
 lanceolata
Koelreuteria paniculata
†*Michelia figo
Magnolia liliiflora
Magnolia × soulangiana
*Nandina domestica
†*Photinia serrulata
*Phyllostachys viridi-
 glaucescens
‡*Rhododendron
 caroliniana
‡*Rhododendron
 ferrugineum
‡*Rhododendron obtusum
Rosa × alba 'Céleste'
Rosa damascena
 'Celsiana'
Rosa gallica 'Tuscany'
Rosa 'Rose d'Amour'

Climbing Roses
Rose 'The Garland'
Rose Félicité et
 Perpétue

Nineteenth-century Flower Gardens
Alstroemeria aurantiaca
Antirrhinum majus
Aquilegia glandulosa
Aster amellus
Aster novae angliae
Campanula carpatica
Campanula lactiflora
†Dahlia coccinea and its
 hybrids
Delphinium grandiflorum
Dianthus Hybrid Pinks
Dicentra spectabilis
Dictamnus albus
Erigeron grandiflorus
Fuchsia magellanica
Galtonia candicans
Geranium sanguineum
Geranium pratense
Gladiolus cardinalis
 illyricus
†Heliotropium
 peruvianum
Hosta lancifolia
Hosta plantaginea

Iris laevigata
Kniphofia uvaria
‡Lilium auratum
‡Lilium tigrinum
Lobelia fulgens
Mimulus variegatus
Oenothera speciosa
†Pelargonium – ivy-
 leaved and zonal
 hybrids
Penstemon campanulatus
Phlox paniculata in
 variety
Romneya coulteri
Salvia involucrata
†Salvia rutilans
Trollius europaeus
Verbena rigida

Arboretums
Acer saccharinum
Betula papyrifera
†*Drimys winteri
Paulownia tomentosa
Quercus palustris
Quercus rubra
Tilia petiolaris
Zelkova carpinifolia

Pinetums
‡*Abies magnifica
*Araucaria araucana
*Cedrus atlantica
*Chamaecyparis
 lawsoniana and in
 variety
*Chamaecyparis obtusa
 and in variety
*Cupressus arizonica
*Cupressus macrocarpa
Ginko biloba
*Juniperus virginiana
*Sequoia sempervirens
*Sequoiadendron
 giganteum
*Picea smithiana
‡*Pinus radiata
*Thuja plicata and in
 variety
‡*Tsuga heterophylla

Rock Gardens
Anemone – see Peat
 Garden
*Arabis albida
‡*Calluna in variety
‡*Cassiope tetragona
*Celmisia coriacea
†*Chamaerops humilis
†*Cordyline australis
Cytisus ardoinii
*Daphne retusa
Dianthus alpinus
Dianthus barbatus
Dryopteris carthusiana
‡*Erica in variety
Genista lydia
Gentiana in variety
Geranium endressii and
 in variety
Iberis saxatilis
Iris chamaeiris
Iris douglasiana
*Juniperus sabina
 tamariscifolia
*Lithospermum diffusum
Osteospermum barberiae
*Phyllitis scolopendrium
*Polypodium vulgare
Polystichum aculeatum
Primula vulgaris in
 variety
Pulsatilla vulgaris
Sedum cauticolum
*Sedum spathulifolium
*Thymus caespititius

Water Gardens
Acer japonicum
*Arundinaria murieliae
Astilbe chinensis 'Pumila'
Astilbe davidii
Betula pendula 'Youngii'
Crocosmia masonorum
Hemerocallis fulva and
 in variety
Hosta decorata
Hosta elata
Iris kaempferi
Iris sibirica
Lysichitum americanum
Miscanthus sinensis
 variegatus

Osmunda regalis
‡Oxydendrum arboreum
Primula japonica in
  variety
Primula 'Bartley Strain'
Primula helodoxa
Rodgersia aesculifolia
  and in variety
Zantedeschia aethiopica

Wild Gardens
Anemone nemorosa and
  in variety
Aster novi-belgii
Caltha palustris
Calystegia sepium var
  americanum
Cyclamen species in
  variety
Erythronium species and
  hybrids in variety
Galanthus nivalis and in
  variety
Hemerocallis in variety
Hydrangea petiolaris
*Iris foetidissima
Leucojum aestivum
Lilium pyrenaicum
Lupinus arboreus
Narcissus species in
  variety
Omphalodes verna
Primula vulgaris in
  variety
Primula elatior
Rosa species in variety
Smilacina racemosa
Solidago virgaurea
Verbascum phlomoides
*Vinca in variety
Wisteria sinensis

Herbaceous and Flower Borders
Abutilon vitifolium
Agapanthus
  campanulatus
†*Artemisia arborescens
Aster × frikartii 'Mönch'
Aster ericoides
*Bergenia cordifolia and
  in variety
‡*Camellia japonica in
  variety
Campanula glomerata
  'Superba'
*Carpenteria californica
Caryopteris ×
  clandonensis
*Ceanothus ×
  veitchianus
Chaenomeles speciosa in
  variety
Clematis montana
Clematis × jackmanii
Clematis 'The President'

‡*Crinodendron
  hookerianum
†Dahlia in variety
Delphinium cheilanthum
*Dianthus 'Mrs Sinkins'
*Euphorbia characias
†*Feijoa sellowiana
Fuchsia 'Enfant
  Prodigue' and in
  variety
Geranium macrorrhizum
Geranium maculatum
Gypsophila paniculata
Helianthus decapetalus
Hydrangea villosa
Iris douglasiana
Iris germanica
*Jasminum humile
  'Revolutum'
Lonicera periclymenum
  'Belgica'
Lupinus arboreus
Magnolia stellata
Nepeta × faassenii
Onopordum acanthium
Perovskia atriplicifolia
*Phlomis fruticosa
Romneya coulteri
†Salvia patens
†Salvia fulgens
*Santolina
  chamaecyparissus
*Senecio 'Sunshine'
Stachys lanata
Tagetes erecta
Verbascum vernale

*Rhododendron species
Rhododendron augustinii
R. barbatum
R. catawbiense
R. caucasicum
R. davidsonianum
R. falconeri
R. fictolacteum
R. griersonianum
R. insigne
R. kiusianum
R. neriiflorum
R. oreotrephes
R. racemosum
R. sutchuenense
R. thomsonii

*Rhododendron Hybrids
Rhododendron 'Beauty of
  Littleworth'
R. 'Brittania'
R. 'Dairymaid'
R. 'Idealist'
R. 'Lady Clementine
  Mitford'
R. 'May Day'
R. 'Purple Splendour'
R. Shilsonii

R. 'Unique'
R. 'Yellow Hammer'

Deciduous Hybrid Azaleas
'Anthony Koster'
'Narcissiflora'
'Spek's Orange'
'Coccinea speciosa'
'Daviesii'

*Japanese and Evergreen Azaleas
'Amoemum'
'Hi-no-mayo'
'Hi-no-degiri'
'Palestrina'

*Hardy Hybrid Rhododendrons suitable for Northern Europe and the coldest parts of North America
'Atrosanguineum'
'Gomer Waterer'
'The Warrior'

Peat Gardens
Anemone blanda in
  variety
Anemone nemorosa in
  variety
Arisaema candidissimum
Arisarum proboscidium
Astilbe simplicifolia
Chionodoxa in variety
Colchicum in variety
‡Cornus canadensis
Crocus species in variety
Cyclamen species in
  variety
Dodecatheon meadia
Epimedium in variety
‡Erica in variety
Erythronium in variety
‡Galax urcedata
‡*Gaultheria cuneata
‡*Gaultheria procumbens
Helleborus in variety
Iris – see Rock Garden
Iris reticulata
‡*Leucothoë catesbaei
Lilium mackliniae
Lilium martagon album
‡Meconopsis betonicifolia
‡Meconopsis grandis
Narcissus species in
  variety
Polygonum affine
Polygonum
  vacciniifolium
Primula florindae
Primula juliae
Primula rosea
‡*Rhododendron
  hanceanum nanum

‡*Rhododendron
  hippophaeoides
‡*Rhododendron
  pemakoense
‡*Rhododendron
  russatum
Salix
*Sarcococca hookeriana
  var digyna
Saxifraga fortunei
Scilla in variety
Tiarella wherryi
Trillium species in
  variety
Uvularia perfoliata
*Vaccinium glauco-album
Viola labradorica
Viola 'Jackanapes'
Viola septentrionalis

Twentieth-century Rose Gardens
Rose 'Caroline Testout'
Rose 'Frau Karl
  Druschki'
  'Shot Silk'

Climbing Roses
R. Albéric 'Barbier'
R. 'Albertine'
R. 'Gloire de Dijon'
R. 'Madame Alfred
  Carrière'
R. 'New Dawn'

Trees and Shrubs in the first part of the Twentieth Century
Acer davidii
Aesculus indica
‡*Camellia japonica in
  variety
‡*Camellia ×
  'Williamsii' in variety
Ceanothus 'Gloire de
  Versailles'
Cedrela sinensis
Cercidiphyllum
  japonicum
Chimonanthus praecox
‡Cornus kousa
‡Corylopsis pauciflora
Corylus maxima
  'Purpurea'
Cotoneaster frigidus
Crataegus prunifolia
Davidia involucrata
*Elaeagnus pungens
  'Maculata'
‡*Embothrium
  longifolium
†*Eucalyptus coccifera
Eucryphia glutinosa
†‡*Eucryphia ×
  'Nymansensis'
Forsythia suspensa

*Garrya elliptica
‡Hamamelis mollis
Hibiscus syriacus
‡Hydrangea macrophylla
  in variety
‡Hydrangea 'Hortensia'
  in variety
Hypericum 'Hidcote'
‡Nothofagus obliqua
†‡*Nothofagus
  cunninghamii
†*Olearia macrodonta
*Osmanthus delavayi
Parrotia persica
Philadelphus 'Belle
  Etoile'
‡*Pieris forrestii
†*Pittosporum
  tenuifolium 'Silver
  Queen'
Prunus subhirtella
  'Autumnalis Rosea'
P. 'Kanzan'
P. 'Shirotae'
P. 'Ukon'
*Senecio rotundifolius
†*Sophora tetraptera
Sorbus aria 'Lutescens'
Sorbus scalaris
*Stranvaesia davidiana
Stuartia pseudo-camellia
‡Styrax japonica
*Viburnum davidii
Viburnum plicatum
  'Mariesii'
Weigela florida
  'Variegata'

5
TOPIARY

There are few gardens of any period in the West which do not owe much of their beauty to topiary. The term topiary, in its broadest sense, refers to any sort of pruning and tending of trees and shrubs; it derives directly from the Latin *topiarius*, a person tending an ornamental garden. Topiary applies as much to fruit trees as to ornamental trees and shrubs, because the very act of pruning a fruit tree to a given shape turns it into an ornamental object. It applies equally to the maintenance of hedges, either surrounding or within the garden, the controlling of trees for screening by pollarding or pleaching, and also, more popularly, the training and clipping of shrubs into geometrical and fancy shapes.

Of whatever form, topiary illustrates the endeavour of man to dominate nature – a dominance which has been carried on by farming, forestry and many other pursuits of today, mostly done with only lip-service to nature's unaided efforts. When building materials were scarce and costly they could be used for the immediate necessities only and thus suitable natural substitutes such as shrubs were used to outline boundaries. In time elaborate designs were being cut into greenery for ornamental purposes, just as stone and metal objects adorned architecture.

Topiary is very much the product of Western civilization. There is little evidence of hedges in records of old gardens in the East. The dividing of a garden into compartments evolved from the use of water canals in Persia and neighbouring countries, and from hedges in Italian gardens. In Italy much use has always been made of plants such as Mediterranean cypresses (*Cupressus sempervirens*), which keep their narrow outline, while others need clipping to achieve the same formal effect.

Topiary became more elaborate in the nineteenth century. Patterns such as peacocks, teddy bears and spirals were popular, as in the Laden garden at Baltimore.

Formal geometric topiary was often placed near the house to reflect architectural features such as windows.

The parterre at Mosely Old Hall, Worcs., is worked in dwarf box on a background of differently graded gravels.

Hedges

Let us consider first the simplest form of topiary, the making and shaping of hedges. It is best to plant only a *single* line of hedging plants. Nothing is gained by planting a double or 'staggered' row; the resulting extra width is always to be avoided. As a rule, a hedge represents in greenery a wall of rectilinear design and thus is clipped with vertical sides and a horizontal top. But this is at variance with the natural shape of all shrubs and is not recommended. The hedge should be wider at the base, tapering inwards slightly to a narrower top.

All sorts of ingenuity can turn the flat lines of a hedge into something more ornamental: at every 2- or 3-metre (6- or 9-foot) interval, for instance, a plant can be grown about 7 to 10 centimetres (3 to 4

inches) wider to represent a buttress, and the leading shoot can gradually be clipped into a sphere, cone or obelisk. Alternatively, the top of the hedge can be clipped into battlements or scallops, or portholes can be cut to give views through the hedge. The buttress idea is sometimes used in a more obvious way: wings can be extended forwards and upwards from the back of the hedge, dividing the border into separate compartments, each perhaps being devoted to a different colour scheme. Here again the wings can have topiary finials or other decoration. These are all ideas which developed as a result of substituting greenery for masonry, which were popular from the seventeenth century onwards. Sometimes the spheres or cones on a holly hedge were made of variegated varieties: this satisfied demands from florists for colour-

Buttressed yews create shady niches for statuary in the Iris garden at Bagatelle.

ful shoots for wreath-making, and the budding of desired varieties on to the leading shoots of a green holly hedge saved ground-space for other crops. This idea was also adopted in private gardens from about 1860 onwards.

Traditional boundary hedges for gardens are made from Quickthorn (*Crataegus monogyna*), Hornbeam (*Carpinus betulus*), Beech (*Fagus sylvatica*), Holly (*Ilex aquifolium*), or Yew (*Taxus baccata*). They all have disadvantages: thorn is very prickly and is usually left for field hedges; hornbeam is less greedy-rooted than beech, but its leaves are of a drab colour in winter and lack beech's warmth (in both, the dead leaves hang on the twigs until the spring); beech suffers from aphids; fallen holly leaves are unpleasant to handle; and yew has poisonous berries.

Dwarf hedges, knot gardens, parterres

Apart from the normal boundary hedge, there are the very small, low hedges or edges used within the garden; and the very tall ones, achieved with trees to create long vistas. While the boundary hedges had their beginnings in the early enclosed garden, these two other categories derive from formal garden design, which grew up after the Renaissance, and particularly in the second half of the seventeenth century in England.

Small beds for flowers were arranged in simple rectangles, initially edged with stone where it was available, or timber or bones, or with dwarf plants such as Thyme (*Thymus vulgaris*), Thrift (*Armeria maritima*), Rosemary (*Rosmarinus officinalis*), Wall Germander (*Teucrium chamaedrys*) and lavenders. In the late seventeenth century these

A hedge in the Laden Topiary Garden, Baltimore, clipped to create 'windows' onto the surrounding countryside.

The silver foliage of Santolina and contrasting annual flowers combine to make a parterre of great charm at La Speranza in Italy.

A knot garden

A knot garden is an ideal feature to bring a sense of history into any small contemporary garden. Popular in the sixteenth and seventeenth centuries, knots are characterized by the intricate interweaving of the ribbon pattern which depends upon the use of contrasting flowers, herbs or foliage for their effect. Geometry is the basis of all knot designs; four knots were usually arranged as a square with sand or gravel paths separating them. This traditional arrangement can, of course, be multiplied to cover a large area.

Originally low-growing herbs such as Hyssop, Thyme, Thrift and *Santolina* were used for knot gardens, all of which can be trimmed into precise lines; later, as a wider range of plants became available, flowers were used, such as different coloured pinks, tulips or hyacinths. Later still, in the seventeenth-century, as evergreens gradually gained in popularity, the outline of the knot pattern was uniformly planted with Dwarf Box, an aromatic plant which is kept in shape by clipping. To add colour to this last type of knot pattern the spaces inside the knot can be filled with different coloured gravels or seasonal flowers.

Whether you choose to make your knot garden from herbs, flowers or Dwarf Box, you will need to decide on a geometric pattern and

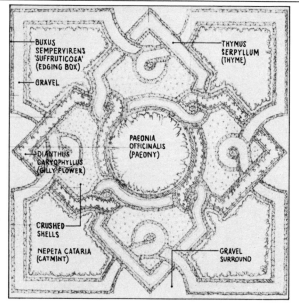

The two knot plans above are from layouts for a proposed restoration in S. Wales.* The designs are based on 'closed knottes' from Lawson's The Country House-Wife's Garden *(1638). The two designs on the right were taken from other gardening manuals of the same period, which provide marvellous inspiration for anyone wishing to make a knot garden.*

*At the Welsh Folk Museum, St. Fagan's Castle, Cardiff.
(Designer Wyn Thomas & Partners, Consultant Paul Edwards.)

The Laburnum arch in full bloom makes an impressive sight at Bodnant in N. Wales.

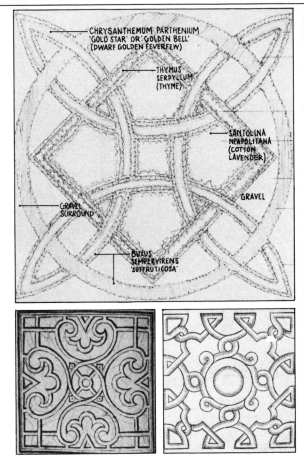

CHRYSANTHEMUM PARTHENIUM
'GOLD STAR' OR 'GOLDEN BELL'
(DWARF GOLDEN FEVERFEW)

THYMUS
SERPYLLUM
(THYME)

SANTOLINA
NEAPOLITANA
(COTTON
LAVENDER)

GRAVEL

GRAVEL
SURROUND

BUXUS
SEMPERVIRENS
'SUFFRUTICOSA'

plot it out to scale on graph paper before laying out the design on well-drained, level ground. Illustrated here are a number of traditional knot patterns – study them to see what was typical of the period, and then copy them or adapt them to your own requirements. You could also invent your own pattern; a fairly simple scheme is usually best.

Once you have chosen your design, draw it carefully to scale on a piece of graph paper. A good size for each knot is 3 × 3 m (10 × 10 ft), although this will obviously vary depending on the space available. Each square on the graph must represent a square on the ground – of 30 × 30 cm (1 × 1 ft) for example – so that the pattern within each square can be faithfully reproduced and pegged out.

Choose compact, low growing perennial plants for the knot. Hyssop, dwarf Lavender, Thyme, *Santolina* and Dwarf Box are all ideal, but there are many other herbs and flowers that could be used – ask your local nursery. A pleasing effect can be achieved by using contrasting colours within the design – the 'Silver Queen' and 'Aureus' varieties of Thyme, for example, would create a striking silver and gold pattern. Buy young plants and plant them fairly close together so that in time they will grow and knit together to form a smooth ribbon.

beds in the ornamental part of the garden developed into intricate patterns, sometimes plainly geometrical, but at times representing the curves of ribbons and bows.

In France the designs became very elaborate, and were copied in England and North America; the edging plants were arranged in great scrolls and arabesques on gravel, and flowering plants were excluded. Differently coloured or variously graded gravels, coal, crushed brick, marble and other materials were used to accentuate the patterns. These patterns created on the ground covered a large level area at the front of the house known as the parterre.

During the late sixteenth century, the Dwarf Box (*Buxus sempervirens* 'Suffruticosa'), which originated in Holland, became the favourite for knot gardens and parterres and has remained so ever since. There is something very satisfying in this contrast of rich green on gravel throughout the year. Sometimes the pattern, best viewed from an upper window, derives as great an appeal when viewed from ground level, where its lines appear to echo the features of the house front. For all knot gardens and parterres it is necessary to start with levelled ground, well drained.

Tall hedges, pollarding and pleaching

Screening of an unsightly view or shelter from wind are sometimes the objectives of a tall hedge today, or its height may have developed through neglect: overgrowth can be the result of insufficiently close clipping. High trestles on wheels are used to clip tall hedges, and even taller contraptions are necessary in tree-pruning in the French manner. In many great French gardens of the seventeenth and eighteenth centuries, long vistas were controlled by an avenue of trees, trimmed flat to a height of

Pleached hornbeams in the Stilt garden at Hidcote, Glos.

some 8 metres (25 feet) and on which the upper branches were allowed to billow over the clipped sides. The control of growth is achieved by the use of long-handled, curved saws and slashers.

A less demanding method of controlling tree screens is by pollarding, which had its origin in the production of poles. The branches of a tree are cut back to some height above the ground to produce a pole, on top of which a rounded head is formed by thick close young growth.

Another practice in the formal gardens of the late seventeenth and early eighteenth centuries was the training of trees, by pollarding and pruning, on to poles and wires to create a screen above a wall or hedge. This is generally termed pleaching. Suitable young, flat-headed trees are planted and tied to tall poles about 3 metres (10 feet) high. Horizontal wires are attached to the poles, 30 cm (1 foot) apart from 2 metres (6 feet) upwards. The tree growths are tied to these wires and pruned annually to achieve the shape desired.

Topiary birds guard the entrance to the bathing pool in Hidcote Manor garden.

Lime (Linden) trees, usually *Tilia platyphyllos* or *T. × euchlora*, are often selected today, but previously *T. × europaea* was the only kind used. Apples and pears also lend themselves to such work. Alternatively, the growths were trained over metal supports to make a tunnel or an arbour. There is a famous tunnel of yews at Melbourne Hall, Derbyshire, in a garden with many examples of topiary.

Low-growing trees or shrubs with hanging flowers, such as laburnum or, in mild maritime districts, *Fuchsia* 'Riccartonii', have been popular since the late nineteenth century. The high clipping of Mediterranean cypresses is a conceit employed also in mild districts, where they may be seen close against house walls, apparently acting as buttresses.

Topiary as Sculpture

The fashion for having stone statuary in gardens derives from ancient Italian gardens. From it evolved the clipping of bushes into geometrical designs and into informal figures; certainly, the geometrical designs are likely to have come first. These pieces, just as if they were stone, may punctuate a design, provide a focal point, serve as a contrast to the free growth of shrubs and plants, or be used in their own right as the *raison d'être* of a portion or the whole of a garden. The greater formal shapes are more often found in big gardens, where they echo the great house, its broad walks and long hedges, masonry features, fountains, balustrading, vases and urns. But nowhere are there exact copies of classical statuary. These formal shapes probably reached the severely formal French and Dutch gardens in the late seventeenth century.

Ornamental topiary went out of fashion during the landscape period of gardening, in the eighteenth century. After Queen Victoria came to the throne in 1837 the art revived considerably, in both formal and informal styles, the inspiration coming from gardens of earlier centuries. Victorian gardening was eclectic and elaborate, and the topiary was likewise elaborate. Fancy shapes – peacocks, teddy bears, spirals, birds-in-ring and the like – were inspired by the Dutch. Some of these may have been planned, or the wayward growth of a shrub may have inspired the owner to shape it over the years into something of normal or fanciful proportions; a harp, for instance, or a railway engine. There is no limit to the shapes that may be achieved in greenery – unless you expect to go directly against nature, such as trying to make a hanging elephant's trunk out of an erect-growing Irish yew. Many topiary pieces appear to be of great age, and, indeed, some date back three or four centuries: there are seventeenth-century specimens

The magnificent topiary gardens at Levens Hall, Cumbria.

A Dutch Garden

The term 'Dutch garden' was coined by gardeners in the nineteenth and early twentieth centuries to designate an area of garden characterized by a compactness of design and the use of topiary, reminiscent of seventeenth-century Dutch gardens. (Confusingly, the style is known in Holland as the 'English garden'). A Dutch garden is therefore a good way to integrate topiary into a relatively small contemporary domestic garden or to create a contained area of specific character within a larger garden, and it would be equally appropriate for a formal town house, a period cottage or a twentieth-century bungalow. A terrace could form the link between house and garden, providing somewhere to eat 'al fresco' meals or sunbathe – for the Dutch garden dispenses with lawns and the tedium of mowing.

Ideally the garden should be enclosed by tall, clipped hedges. If the ground has been thoroughly prepared and the boundary hedges fed and trimmed regularly, they should reach their full height fairly quickly.

The most sympathetic material to use for the paths of a Dutch garden is brick laid in basket-weave or herringbone pattern; its warm colour will accentuate the sharp green of the box topiary.

Keep the outline of flowerbeds simple and the planting relatively low-growing to allow the topiary to be the dominant feature of the garden. Border the beds with the soft grey of lavender (Dutch Lavender [*L. vera*] is ideal for this purpose), and fill them with white roses, as Gertrude Jekyll did in the Dutch Garden at 'Orchards' in Surrey. These could be underplanted with silvery *Stachys lanata* or pale snapdragons (*Antirrhinum*). In spring the garden would provide a splendid setting for a massed display of tulips or hyacinths.

Make your Box topiary features at the axes of the paths, establishing a firm base before developing a lead shoot to make a smooth finial or perhaps something figurative, like fan-tail doves. Although it will take patience your 'Dutch' garden, once established, will be something of interest and beauty for generations.

in the remarkable topiary garden at Levens Hall, Cumbria, at Rous Lench Court, Worcestershire, and the 9-metre (30-feet) high pyramids under the walls of Powis Castle, Wales, which started life as small trees about a fifth of the size. However, much apparently ancient topiary was started in the late nineteenth century, as at Compton Wynyates in Warwickshire, Chirk Castle, Clwyd, and the multitude of yews at Packwood House, Warwickshire (only the big yews at the top of this garden date from earlier times).

John Evelyn, the diarist, in 1662 called attention to the excellence of the English Yew for garden work. It has remained the favourite for topiary ever since. Yew is evergreen, sturdy, stands clipping well and thrives on any reasonably drained soil. Common Box (*Buxus sempervirens*), another native of Britain and Europe, has been used also, but tends to lose its rigidity: its branches sag when they have too great a weight of foliage and twigs to support. It is, however, a much fresher green than the sombre yew. Hornbeam and Beech, though useful, are rather too coarse in growth for finished work.

Creating Topiary

There are several ways of making topiary pieces. One is the time-honoured, but slow, method of gradually clipping a finial, sphere or fancy shape into the form re-

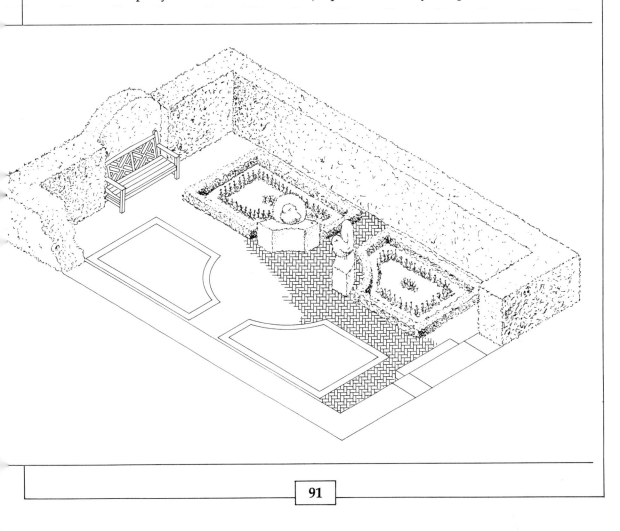

Growing Topiary

To create large topiary features fairly quickly it is often best to use several cuttings closely planted so that they grow together and encourage each other up. Three plants would give a good start to a cone or globe, four to an obelisk, and five (one a central, larger, plant) for any design in which a tall element rises above a square cut base.

Plants should be raised from cuttings all taken from the same clone, as this will ensure that they all grow at the same rate. Common Box (*Buxus sempervirens*) is perhaps the most popular plant for small topiary; yews are more suitable for large specimens.

Prepare the ground really well before planting, and feed the plants amply to ensure luxuriant and constant growth. Remember that clipping reduces a plant's ability to take in goodness from the sun, and this goodness has to be replaced. Do not start to clip a plant until it is at least two years old.

As the plants grow, examine the branch formation carefully to discover what basic outline the plant most resembles. Do not try to force a plant into a shape contrary to a growing pattern. Be flexible; if you see a healthy bush suited to a spiral or pyramid, forget the teddy bear you had planned.

MAKING A PEACOCK
Basic requirements
Stout galvanized wire
Strong garden twine
Pair of pliers
Two natural canes
Six green canes
One or more healthy bush(es) planted at its permanent site or in a container.

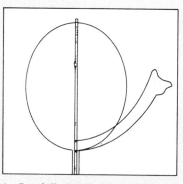

1. Carefully bend the wire into the desired shape with pliers, allowing 15 cm (6 inches) of wire at the base to act as an anchor in the soil. Tie a natural cane to the wire frame so that it is in line with the anchor.

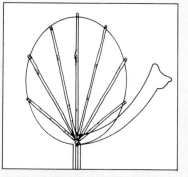

2. Tie green canes on to the circular frame in a fan shape. Fan them out from the wire and cane base.

DO
– make sure that both natural canes are treated with tar or Solignum for at least six inches at the end which will be in the soil. Rotten canes will fall over.
– feed the bush with fertilizer; once in spring at the beginning of the growing season, and again using bone meal after clipping in

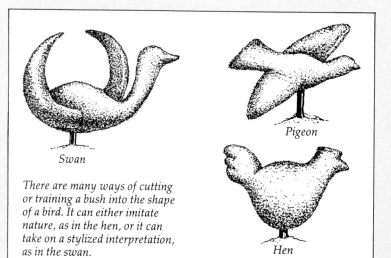

Swan

Pigeon

Hen

There are many ways of cutting or training a bush into the shape of a bird. It can either imitate nature, as in the hen, or it can take on a stylized interpretation, as in the swan.

the autumn as a tonic for the winter.

– allow as many branches as possible to grow in the first five years. These can be worked into the main design and will add both density and dimension to the shape.

– protect the topiary from strong or winter winds with a temporary wind shield.

– shake off snow which lies on the branches and if necessary add a frame to prevent the branches breaking or distorting.

DO NOT

– clip or cut off any branches for the first two years. Give the root system time to

establish itself firmly to ensure rapid and healthy growth above ground.

– allow the bush to dry out in its first three years. During long hot spells water alternately at the base and on the foliage.

– cut off leading shoots until satisfied that the height and shape are correct.

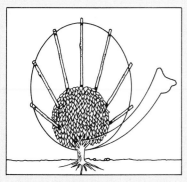

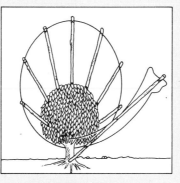

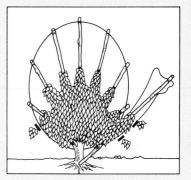

3. Place the frame over the bush and firm it into place. Take care not to damage the root system with the anchor.

4. Work the second natural cane along the wire neck and into the base of the bush, as near the anchor as possible. Tie it into place in at least two points.

5. Arrange the branches on the frame and tie them in to place. Do not tie too tightly at this stage as the branches are still young; allow for firmer training during the next growing season.

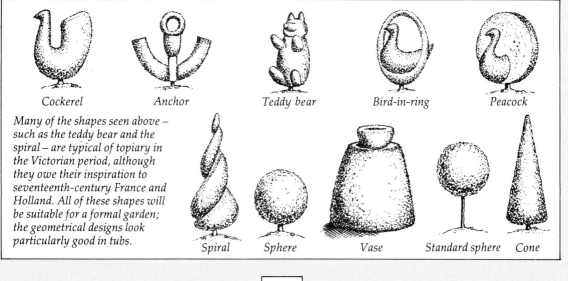

Cockerel *Anchor* *Teddy bear* *Bird-in-ring* *Peacock*

Many of the shapes seen above – such as the teddy bear and the spiral – are typical of topiary in the Victorian period, although they owe their inspiration to seventeenth-century France and Holland. All of these shapes will be suitable for a formal garden; the geometrical designs look particularly good in tubs.

Spiral *Sphere* *Vase* *Standard sphere* *Cone*

quired. It takes a lot of patience. But there are two methods which save time. One is to plant several bushes of the required different sizes together, to make the basic formal shape. This was done with yews to fill a gap in a formal array of topiary pieces in the Long Garden at Cliveden, Berkshire, and also for the large specimens at the entrance to the American Cemetery at Brookwood, Woking, Surrey. But unfortunately yews are generally raised from seeds, with a resultant variation in growth, which becomes apparent after some years of clipping. Common Box, however, is usually raised from cuttings and, provided the plants are of one particular clone, this trouble does not arise. The same applies to seed-raised hollies as opposed to vegetatively propagated forms.

In order to make a topiary piece quickly from one plant it is necessary to give it ample feeding and attention so that it grows luxuriantly. Then, when it has reached the required height, its mode of branching must be examined carefully, to decide which shape suits it best. Unwanted branches can then be removed and the use of stakes and wire will guide the selected growths into their right positions. After four or five years of tending, tying, pinching out and clipping, an apparently 'old' specimen will be achieved.

The work of clipping can be done with hand shears, secateurs or electric cutters. Today most workers use the latter. Yew is generally clipped, along with most hedges, in late summer; Box can be done at the same time, but immediately after the summer's first growth is preferable. The act of clipping reduces the plant's ability to take in goodness from the sun. As with lawns, this loss has to be replaced by feeding. A general fertilizer every two years is usually enough, but very old hedges are often

infested with ivy and weeds, which should be removed before feeding.

However closely a plant is cut, a little of the season's growth remains each year. This means that hedges and other topiary get steadily wider, and so, with age, sometimes become rather clumsy, losing their pristine charm, and it is very difficult to reduce them.

For all types of clipping, it is a good idea to lay a large cloth on the ground before starting; this is to catch the leaves. Shears

The elaborate Laurel maze at Glendurgan, in Cornwall, was planted in 1833 and is still maintained today.

are quite suitable for small-leafed shrubs such as yew and box, but holly, Portuguese Laurel and other broad-leafed evergreens are best managed with secateurs.

Training of Fruit Trees

Topiary in the kitchen garden is usually in the form of trained fruit trees. Many old gardens still boast well-trained peaches, pears, apples and plums, either fan-trained on walls or free-standing espaliers. Much more popular today would be the apples and pears on extra dwarfing root-stocks from which interesting shapes can be made. These trees normally do not exceed 2 metres (6 feet) in height, which means easy pruning, spraying, thinning and picking. The French are renowned for their mastery of this art, and their favoured shapes include pyramids and cordons, as well as more fanciful ones: vases, for instance, or hoops or swags. Pruning deciduous trees, such as fruit trees and limes (lindens), is best done during open weather in winter.

Mazes

The simplest form of maze is one where the intricate and confusing lines are paths cut out of level turf. The underlying idea of hedged mazes seems to be connected with life and religion, with the goal at the centre of things.

To be really successful the hedges of a maze should be dense and thick and higher than the average human; moreover, to increase the difficulty and mystery, a one-person-wide passage is the ideal. The narrowness and height of such a path necessitate the choice of a shrub which will grow well regardless of shade; for this, the yew is particularly suited.

A design for a maze, published in 1583 by de Vries.

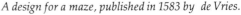

An engraving (1726) showing early methods of cultivation.

6
KITCHEN GARDENS

The Romans were skilled in the cultivation of food crops and their influence was strong in much of Europe; the edible plants they cultivated throughout their empire included lettuce, endive, leeks, onions, garlic, cabbage, broad beans, globe artichoke and asparagus. They grew vines, apples, pears, figs and nuts and appreciated that some pruning and removal of dead wood increased the cropping potential. Their herbal knowledge was based upon plants indigenous to the Mediterranean regions – indeed European herbal knowledge centred around these plants until Renaissance times.

The Romans introduced some of these herbs into northern Europe – nettles and lavender, for example – to add to the plants native to the temperate regions, such as sorrel, celery, seakale, parsnip, thyme, chamomile and comfrey. Many of the plants they introduced became sufficiently acclimatized to survive as naturalized plants; the remainder were reintroduced much later.

Monastic settlements all over Europe renewed the attention to cultivation methods; during the Middle Ages monks became the custodians of both plants and horticultural skills. Some rotation of crops was practised allowing a three-year rotation, including a fallow area to allow the soil to recover. But it was not until the early eighteenth century that any significant scientific study was made of nutrients and their relationship to different crops.

The science of horticulture developed following the arrival in Europe of the more exotic food plants from the New World. European gardens were gradually enriched by kidney and 'French' beans, scarlet runner beans, red peppers, lima beans, pineapples, potatoes and tomatoes. And it became fashionable to use labour-intensive methods of forcing to extend the season, and plant vegetables in regimented formality. The Dutch and Flemish were especially inventive in contriving methods of forcing and protection: it is said that they could supply all the courts of Europe with fresh fruit in the seventeenth and eighteenth centuries.

The Potager

The French *potager* was developed from a series of beds forming a pleasing pattern and filled with vegetables. Once the great gardens of Versailles were complete (about 1678), Jean de la Quintinye was commissioned to lay out a grand kitchen garden, or *potager*, for Louis XIV. Such a garden had existed previously, but had been overrun by the general design of the new *parc*.

The huge site was enclosed by high walls, and bays and terraces were formed to afford shelter. By using lights, glass-houses and 'heating' devices, out-of-season asparagus, strawberries, figs, melons and radishes were produced for the royal household. Individual beds were protected by low hedges, fruit trees were grown in pots and, above all, La Quintinye developed a system of growing fruit trees against the walls and pruning them to increase the crops.

European Settlers in the New World

The early American settlers appear to have grown both fruit and vegetables in a comparatively haphazard way, in spite of the horticultural expertise they must have been familiar with in Europe. Livestock was often kept beneath fruit trees, and most reports seem to stress that herbs were grown mainly for the alleviation of sickness.

William Wood and John Josselyn both recorded the plants cultivated in New England gardens about 1630. According to Wood in his *New England Prospect* (1633): 'The ground affords very good kitchen

A garden plan from Batty Langley's 'New Principles of Gardening', 1728.

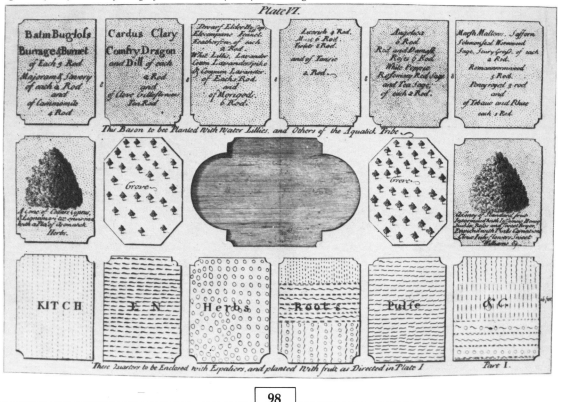

gardens for Turneps, Parsnips, Carrots, Radishes and Pompions, Muskmillons, Isquoter squashes, coucumbers, Onyons, and whatever grows well in England grows well there, many things being better and larger: there is likewise growing all manner of Hearbes for meate and medicine, and that not only in planted Gardens, but in the Woods without either the art of helpe of man, as sweet Marjoran, Purslane, Sorrell, Penneriall, Yarrow, Mirtle, Saxifarilla, Bayes, etc.'

Correspondence with the homelands in Europe reveals requests for seeds and for detailed knowledge of herbal remedies. Governor William Bradford of the Plymouth Plantation committed his descriptions of the plants the settlers were growing to verse:

> All sorts of roots and herbes in gardens grow,
> Parsnips, carrots, turnips or what you'll sow,
> Onions, melons, cucumbers, radishes,
> Skirrets, beets, coleworts and fair cabbages.
> Here grow fine flowers many and mongst those,
> The fair white lily and the sweet fragrant rose.
>
> Many good wholesome berries here you'll find,
> Fit for men's use, almost of every kind,
> Pears, apples, cherries, plumbs, quinces and peach,
> Are now no dainties; you may have of each.
> Nuts and grapes of several sorts are here,
> If you will take the pains them to seek for.'

Little seems to have been recorded of these early gardens; obviously food was the prime requirement and it is unlikely that elaborate layouts existed. The tomato, potato, and capsicum were not yet known, and even when they were, seem to have been cultivated far more in Europe than in America.

It is from the garden books of both Washington and Jefferson that concrete information comes. Both their gardens – Washington's at Mount Vernon and Jefferson's at Monticello – have recently been reconstructed, so the would-be period

gardener has ready-made examples of eighteenth-century gardens in the USA. In both plans the kitchen garden plays a significant role. Jefferson was particularly interested in his, and was one of the first people to cultivate the tomato in America. He had almost twenty kinds of English peas – his favourite vegetable.

Vegetables and Herbs

Through all the changing tastes and fashions of gardens, the kitchen garden has remained singularly timeless in its trim rigidity – and this for good reason. The vegetable- and herb-growing seasons are short and, in order to produce the maximum in the time, the crops are planted closely, usually in rows. Such a mathematical approach provides some shelter

Washington's kitchen garden at Mount Vernon was first created in 1786 and restored in 1936.

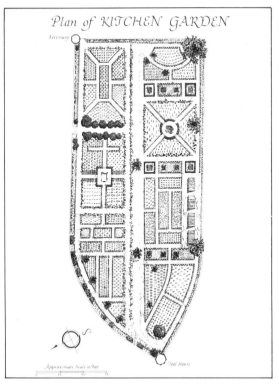

among the crops themselves, ensures tidiness and economy, allows each plant its allotted growing space, and gives the gardener some measure of control.

From medieval times, produce gardens were always depicted as a series of rectangular beds amid sanded paths, and usually the bed contained just one kind of vegetable: cabbage, for instance, or artichoke or beans. Sometimes, two differing vegetables were shown, often a lettuce-type crop interplanted with onions. Probably the lettuce formed what, today, would be termed a catch crop.

Beds were often small, to allow easy access from all sides, and were raised, to improve the drainage of surface water. The sides were supported with wood boards, a practice that survived until early in the present century. In the intervening period, special tiles for supporting edges were manufactured, especially in nineteenth-century England, and trim box-edging became customary. This in itself was but a variation of the French or Dutch *potager* where beds were edged or outlined, quite frequently, by small clipped hedges or even low trellises.

The relative size of the individual beds has increased over the last 300 years, partly to enlarge the area to be cultivated and, more recently, to allow for mechanization. The rectilinear plan has remained, usually with some sort of surrounding wall or fence. Beds at the base of these walls were usually sown with the perennial vegetables such as asparagus or artichokes. Sometimes, especially in the seventeenth and eighteenth centuries, the beds were banked against the wall to catch more sunshine for the production of early crops. Then they began to be covered with lights, of oiled paper or glass, to offer more protection and to encourage earlier maturity. Occasionally,

Tomatoes, illustrated here in Gerard's 'Herbal' of 1633, were given the curious name 'Apples of Love'.

individual plants such as melons were depicted in contemporary French and German illustration as being protected by cloches or some other form of hand light.

Crops

In the present century a clear distinction is made between vegetable crops and herbs, but it was only during the first two or three decades of this century that herbs came to be cultivated in separate decorative gardens. Salad crops, or 'sallets', was a term for all leaf vegetables including those now defined as herbs, while 'roots' was the prevalent term for other crops. The word

A plate from Gerard's 'Herbal' of 1633 shows how different garden lettuce was then.

'vegetable' came into use as a blanket term during the eighteenth century.

All over Europe in the seventeenth century an extensive range of vegetables was grown: some of which were used in ways now obsolete. For example, the leaves removed from overwintering roots were eaten, seedlings and thinnings were gathered as fresh food, and such plants as Cleavers (*Galium aparine*), Good King Henry (*Chenopodium bonus-henricus*), Scurvy Grass (*Cochlearia officinalis*), Comfrey (*Symphytum officinalis*) and Alexanders (*Smyrnium olusatrum*) were cultivated. Regional variations were much more pronounced than today, influenced by climate and soil and by epicurean preferences. Globe Artichokes, varying in colour from deep pink through green to white – some pointed, others round, some tall growing, others short – were grown in Italy and France, and remain popular there. Henry VIII tried to encourage their cultivation in England by establishing his 'Hartichoake' garden, but without success.

The practice of growing and blanching the artichokes for winter use has fallen into disuse. Cardoons, closely related to globe artichokes, were given this treatment too; they have remained a French and Flemish vegetable delight. John Tradescant reported seeing three acres of them near Brussels, blanched for winter use. The other artichoke, the Jerusalem, when newly introduced from across the Atlantic in the sixteenth century, was first called Canadian Potato. Two more types of potatoes first grown in Europe at about the same time were the 'Virginian', which, updated, is still cultivated today, and the Sweet Potato, which became far more popular in southern Europe than in the north.

Cauliflowers, originally from Cyprus but with a fecund background through several European countries, gradually spread north, along with the broccoli and other brassicas. Coleworts and cabbages, especially red cabbage, were salad vegetables, as was raw cauliflower, which was often pickled in brine. The Flemish improved the cultivation of the cauliflower, and from there it was introduced into England in the sixteenth century. It did not have the firm, round-headed 'flowers' of today, but was leafier and looser in the curd.

Savoys, cabbage and kale (all classed as coleworts), sorrel, endive (especially in France and the Low Countries) and spinach formed the basis of leaf crops. New

Zealand spinach arrived via Australia in the eighteenth century. It is interesting to note that the growing of kale was more popularly practised in northern Europe. Sometimes coarse in texture, and usually considered as fodder, it is still used in northern England and Scotland as a good hardy winter leaf crop.

Onions were of considerable importance, providing a range of flavours, and in sixteenth-century England were said to be the most popular vegetable, occupying more growing land than any other. They could be pulled as spring onions, and included shallots, leeks, garlic, rampion and rocambole. Celery, seakale, beet, tansy, purslane and mint were native plants of northern Europe and were each taken into cultivation. An assortment of peas, tall or dwarf-growing, seems to have existed, no doubt cross-fertilizing. A wide variety of beans, too, was available. Many pulses were stored for winter use or gathered at an immature stage and cooked complete with pods.

Variety

Local variations developed through the saving of seed from one crop to the next, producing what today would be known as a 'land race' or 'land strain'. Even until very recent times, such land strains represented a rich diversity within a given type of one vegetable. (Undoubtedly, it is because of the quality of available seed that modern vegetable gardening supersedes that of former centuries.) Obviously, the sturdiest land strains survived; and those with virus infection and other deficiencies were gradually abandoned. It is therefore impossible to say precisely what was grown in any particular segment of time. The date of plant introductions does not necessarily mean that the plants were commercially available or widely grown from that time.

The would-be period kitchen gardener, then, has to depend upon older methods of cultivation, cumbersome and antiquated methods of producing early crops or extending the season, and a total adherance to organic sprays and manures. The use of bulky organic manures such as dung, spent hops, shoddy or seaweed; the value of soft soap as an insecticide, naphthalene or derris sprays, pyrethrum dust; and the older beliefs of companion planting and astrological gardening should be studied in specialist books and older gardening manuals, especially those relating to the period to be recreated.

Digging

The digging of ground in which vegetables were to be cultivated became common horticultural practice in the Low Countries during the fifteenth and sixteenth centuries. It was the Huguenot refugees, many of them highly skilled market gardeners, who introduced the custom into England and Denmark. William Lawson wrote in 1617 that landlords who leased their land to the refugees were afraid 'they would spoil the ground because they did use to dig it'. But results must have justified the efforts: digging in preparation for vegetable cultivation soon became standard practice. From the eighteenth to the first half of the present century, the labour-intensive, time-consuming operations of trenching, double trenching, ridging (particularly on heavy soils) and digging over as opposed to forking over, were all a regular part of ground preparation. It is mainly in northern Europe that digging has played such an important role; on the thinner soils of southern Europe the mattock is the universal tool, as opposed to the fork and spade elsewhere.

Old terracotta forcing pots can still be found.

Forcing

When plants are grown quickly and harvested earlier than normal, they are described as 'forced'. Some salad crops, particularly lettuce, endive, chicory and mint, lend themselves to such treatment, particularly when grown under glass. Some are forced or merely blanched better in darkness, notably seakale and rhubarb, both of which were forced out of doors under special earthenware pots. These are sometimes seen in old gardens, and estate sales, jumble sales and junk yards may well be good hunting grounds for those gardeners who wish to acquire them. Upturned buckets, the bottoms pierced in one or two places, provide the same results, or clay chimney pots are sometimes used.

The forcing of a vegetable crop, or merely the hastening of the germination process or seedling stage, captured the interest of both Dutch and French kitchen gardeners. The Dutch produced early salad crops better than anyone else and supplied them to the other countries of Europe. The French, on the other hand, used a system of intensive cultivation, incorporating the use of frames, cloches and hot beds, critically timed catch crops, and intercropping: the French kitchen garden area emulated a factory production line. The combination of this and espaliered fruit trees, which allow more space and light for vegetables, is perhaps what the period gardener could aim for.

Intensive cultivation, imitative of the methods of the last three centuries, needs to be investigated carefully before being used. Obviously a kitchen garden as large as those of the past would be expensive, but a small, intensively cropped area often produces excellent results. Modern varieties of vegetables can be used to give an extended season with the old cultural methods.

Cloches

Bell glasses and cloches serve quite a different purpose from the modern plastic cloche. The latter merely affords protection and is not a forcing device.

The glass cloche creates a total microclimate, with high light intensity; when used in conjunction with a hot bed it needs careful management. Originally bell shaped, hence the French name *cloche*, meaning a bell, it is thought to have been used first by the Dutch, the first gardeners to cover individual plants with glass structures. Old handlights, as they were prosaically called in English, are difficult to reconstruct. Square or rectangular designs, with some sort of a handle at the apex, were the most popular in England, while the Dutch and French preferred the rounded ones; both kinds were composed of many panes of glass. Bell glasses are sometimes to be found in estate sales and old gardens, but their life is limited – one

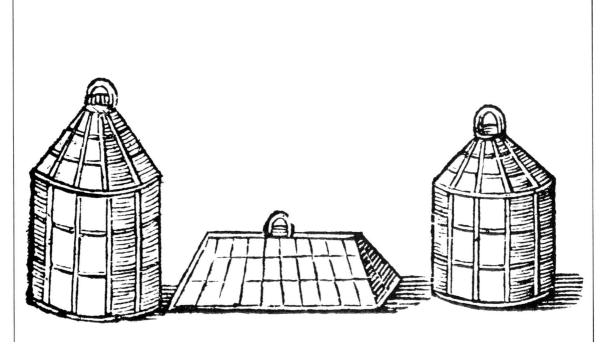

Seventeenth-century Dutch handlights. Illustration from 'Den Nederlandtsen Hovenier', 1683.

crack and they shatter. It is far more likely that the old handlight or 'lantern' style can be found, as individual broken panes are repairable.

When positioning the cloche, often a couple of small depressions are made in the soil beneath the rim to allow some ventilation, although for crops such as cos lettuce, which need more air than cabbage lettuce, the whole glass can be tipped up and wedged by a stone. Wooden pegs used to be made for this purpose, notched at intervals, and they also served to keep open the lights on frames. To prevent the 'burning' of crops below the cloches the glass can be limewashed, and it used to be customary to knock off the surmounting glass knob or handle to prevent it acting as a lens.

There were elaborate systems of 'cloche moving', whereby cabbage and cos lettuce, for example, could be grown together through the winter over a hot bed. Once the cabbage lettuces had been cut the cloches were moved a short distance across to bring on the later cos. The almost mathematical routines evolved for moving cloches among crops resembled some great game of chess. The nineteenth-century kitchen garden manuals suggested variations and routines that could be tried.

Hot Beds

The hot bed has been known since Roman times as a method of warming soil to encourage the production of out-of-season crops. It was widely used all over Europe during the eighteenth century for the growing of pineapples – or pines as they were called.

Such beds are based on the heat produced by the fermentation of horse manure (tanbark, bark used in tanning, was used in

Handlights like these can still be found today in auctions and sale rooms. Broken panes are easy to repair.

the past). Ideally, horse manure from racing or military stables is best, free from disinfectants and mixed with clean short straw. Farmyard manure incorporating straw is a second possibility, but it ought to contain a fair proportion of horse dung. In comparison, cow manure is cold, and pig manure colder still. Dung should be collected during the summer and early autumn and stored in piles under cover. (Kitchen gardens used to have a covered paved area, with drainage channels, as a special storage area.) In the past, management of a dung heap destined for hot-bed use was no casual affair. The French were very particular, and even kept long- and short-straw dung stacked separately.

If patches of white fungus appear, signifying overheating, the straw can be cooled by either turning, adding leaf mould or autumn leaves, or by splitting the heap into two with a pitch or dung fork. Turning the heap helps to keep the temperature even. The amount of moisture is a matter for trial and error; some will drain away and some will evaporate as steam once the heap warms up. The texture should never become too dry and crumbly.

The material ought to be ready for use by mid-winter, and a temperature of as much as 32°C (90°F) can be obtained, although a little lower is adequate for hot beds. Fresh material is mixed with old hot-bed material, or a black crumbly substance called *terreau*, or with old mushroom compost. The mixing and incorporating will, in itself, reduce the temperature. The material is then taken to the position in which the crops are to be cultivated, formed into a 'bed' and spread with top soil. It is then allowed to warm up under frame lights before cultivation begins.

Frames

The hot bed of fermenting manure is seldom used today for providing bottom heat in a garden frame. Two principal methods of managing frames over hot beds are the Dutch and the English. The latter is more extravagant with hot-bed material, but has the advantage that the heat is perfectly even over the whole soil surface. Material is built up into raised beds 45 to 60 cm (18 to 24 inches) high, and of a convenient size and length to take a number of frames, allowing an extension of 30.5 cm (12 inches) outside the frame in each direction. Soil to the depth of about 20.5 cm (8 inches) is then packed over the hot-bed material, and a wooden frame placed in position. Either Dutch or French lights were used in this English method. The Dutch method involves more preparatory time and effort, but uses less hot-bed material. A cavity or trench is made about 60 cm (2 feet) wide and deep and as long as necessary to fit the required number of frames. It is then filled with hot-bed material, and covered with about 20.5 cm (8 inches) of soil acquired during the excavation. The top soil surface should have a slight slope, if possible towards the south (or north in the Southern Hemisphere) – the trench should be dug roughly from east to west (or the reverse in the Southern Hemisphere) – because the heat is considered to be better conserved in this method of preparation. Sometimes an alleyway is dug out immediately behind the frame and filled with straw, to help the drainage within the frame.

The lights used to cover such frames were opened a little on warm days, supported by wood pegs, to maintain a buoyant atmosphere inside the frame. Otherwise it was general practice to close and cover the lights with mats as soon as darkness fell, in order to conserve as much heat as possible. The mats were woven from strips of fibre or the inner bark of the lime tree and were imported from Archangel, Russia. Nowadays, hessian or coconut-fibre matting would suffice.

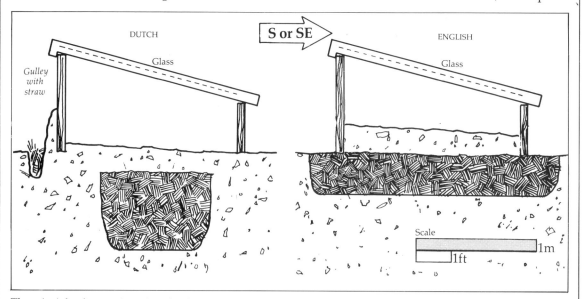

The principle of a Dutch method hot bed is similar to that of the English.

Herb Gardens

Colloquially, the word 'herb' has come to mean a plant employed for its flavour, fragrance or healing quality. Physic gardens have existed since very early times all over Europe, attached to hospices, monasteries and medical schools, and in recent centuries sometimes as part of botanic gardens. Old books refer to 'herbes' or 'herbys' cultivated for flavour and household remedies, and today several of them are regarded as vegetables: cucumbers, leeks, onions, garlic, orache, radishes and cornsalad.

Batty Langley, in his *New Principles of Gardening* (1728), when naming 'Herbs as are absolutely necessary for the service of all Gentlemen and other Families in general', produced a long list of plants, all of which were accommodated in his proposed kitchen garden. For the next 150 years, herbs were cultivated as part of the kitchen garden, although they waned in importance throughout the nineteenth century and were often grown as pot herbs, garnishing and sweet herbs. The so-called 'traditional' herb garden so popular today in England and America – but never catching on in mainland Europe – is certainly not a reflection of any earlier style: the plants are traditional, but there the similarity ends.

Thus, the period gardener, unless seeking to emulate the 1920s and 1930s, need look no further for the design of herb gardens than the medieval chequerboard pattern. Alternate squares are planted; the others are paved, sanded or planted with chamomile or pennyroyal to provide scented underfooting. Each planted square ought to contain only one kind of herb, as in the medieval practice.

The 'traditional' herb garden seems to have been originated by Gertrude Jekyll.

Writing in 1900 in *Home and Garden*, she included herbs in the kitchen garden, but during the following decade she isolated the herb garden as a decorative feature in the garden itself. In 1907, for Knebworth, Hertfordshire, she designed a simple herb garden based on five circles, immediately outside the kitchen garden wall – almost as if these old plants were being introduced to the outside world. The garden was not made in her lifetime, but recently has been laid out according to her design. Today

A collection of thymes planted in the chequerboard style, popular in the 1920s and '30s.

every sweet-scented plant is included in a herb garden, which is more closely related to the knot garden of the sixteenth century. But the knot was a decorative feature, and the herbs it was composed of were not harvested.

In America, herb gardens made during the past twenty years are very similar to those popular in England. The Western Reserve Herb Garden at Cleveland, Ohio, is one of the best, and there is another good example at the Chicago Horticultural Society's Botanic Garden in Glencoe, Illinois.

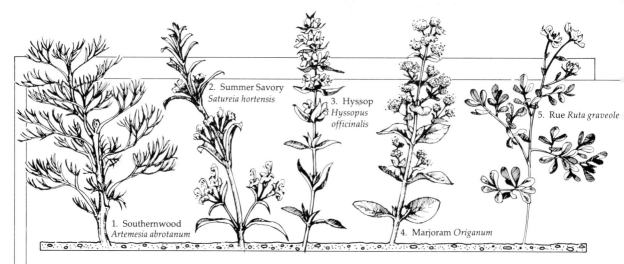

2. Summer Savory
Satureia hortensis

3. Hyssop
Hyssopus officinalis

5. Rue *Ruta graveole*

1. Southernwood
Artemesia abrotanum

4. Marjoram *Origanum*

An Edwardian Herb Garden

During the early part of this century there was a resurgent interest in herb growing such as there had not been since medieval times. This may, in part, have been due to a new awareness of the diversity of form and colour to be found in foliage plants, a concept reawakened in the UK by the work of Jekyll and continued by Vita Sackville-West. But although it was aesthetic rather than utilitarian motives which prompted the popularity of herb gardens, to have an abundant supply of fresh herbs is certainly an additional pleasure.

A herb garden need not be very large – even a single bed would suffice – but there are so many different herbs that it would not be difficult to fill an entire garden with them. Besides the most familiar, culinary herbs such as parsley, mint, thyme and rosemary, there is a host of other, lesser known, plants which deserve inclusion, such as the time revered Apothecary's Rose (*R. gallica*), aromatic

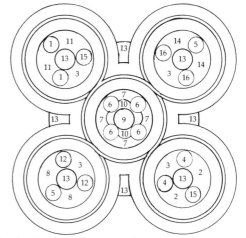

The plan for the herb garden above was designed in 1907 by Gertrude Jekyll for the Earl of Lytton at Knebworth House, Herts. At that time it was not constructed, but it has recently been built to Jekyll's original specification. Knebworth House is open to the public during the summer.

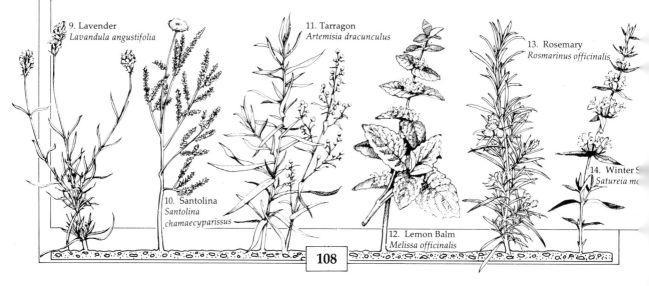

9. Lavender
Lavandula angustifolia

11. Tarragon
Artemisia dracunculus

13. Rosemary
Rosmarinus officinalis

10. Santolina
Santolina chamaecyparissus

12. Lemon Balm
Melissa officinalis

14. Winter S
Satureia m

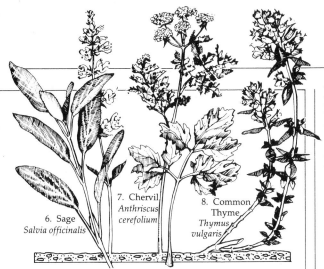

6. Sage
Salvia officinalis

7. Chervil
Anthriscus cerefolium

8. Common Thyme
Thymus vulgaris

Southernwood (*Artemisia abrotanum*), Borage (*Borago officinalis*) with its clear blue flowers and the delicate fronds of bronze Fennel. Instead of confining herbs to the beds, make more of them: allow Honeysuckle to scramble over the walls and use Hops to make a shady arbour; plant Wild Strawberries as ground cover and decorate the garden with terracotta pots overflowing with nasturtiums. Plant the tiny *Menta requienii* or *Thymus drucei* 'Minus' in the cracks between paving stones, and make a fragrant seat of Chamomile.

Given the right conditions herbs grow and spread very rapidly. Many may be grown from seed, so a herb garden can be quickly and inexpensively established and will actually benefit from regular harvesting.

Edwardian herb gardens were usually formal in style and frequently surrounded by protective hedges. You can design a herb garden to any pattern you choose, or you can copy or adapt Gertrude Jekyll's plan for the herb garden at Knebworth house shown here.

16. Horehound
Marrubium vulgare

17. Fennel
Foeniculum vulgare

15. Alecost
Tanacetum balsamita

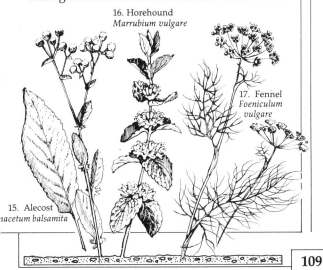

Fruit Growing

Fruit has generally been incorporated into the kitchen garden and not allocated an exclusive plot. Cottage and villa gardens have often included a fruit tree – in northern Europe a plum or apple, in France a pear, and in Austria and Italy a cherry or apricot. In the foothills of the European mountains from the Tatra to the Pyrenees, peasant and landlord alike have always maintained a small vineyard, usually planted on terraced south-facing slopes.

Bunches of grapes on a wall-trained vine are individually protected in this Italian garden.

From the seventeenth to the early twentieth century in France and Holland, and in the nineteenth century in England, the intensive cultivation of fruit in the kitchen gardens became almost a fetish. When fruit trees and fruit scions became international horticultural currency in Europe, many seeds were sent to the New World. There, enormous numbers of seedlings were grown, and many competent gardeners practised grafting. By the time the first commercial catalogues appeared in America nearly all the varieties offered were home developments. Some of these are still grown today.

Intensive Cultivation

Fortunately for the would-be period gardener, the intensive fruit cultivation systems commend themselves to the small modern garden. In northern Europe in the late seventeenth and early eighteenth centuries, the failure to grow successful pineapples, oranges, bananas and pomegranates led to a general decline in fruit cultivation, except in France. But in the two decades from 1780 there was a tremendous upsurge in available varieties. The pruning and training of so-called 'top fruit' became particularly important: cordon, oblique cordon, double cordon, pillar, espalier, fan, goblet, and, in France and Belgium, *l'arcure* systems were all practised. Soft fruit, also, was trained to enhance the crop and reduce leaf formation. Gooseberries and currants as cordons and standards, raspberries latticed to supports for control, strawberries grown in blocks – often on south-facing sloping beds or in barrels – were all essential parts of the potager and kitchen garden.

Pruning and training is a slow process even for the most patient of gardeners. But the festooning of a limited number of leaders for a year or two when young, with the best bud at the top, will provide a basic form of intensive cultivation. For apples, tip-bearing or biennial-bearing varieties should be avoided, and, in general, the modern dwarfing rootstocks (some of them virus free) now available for most fruits, including plums, are particularly useful. Nurseries specializing in fruit will always advise on suitable varieties, and some old varieties are becoming available.

Once established, intensive fruit cultivation can be easily confined within netting to protect against birds, and usually one good tar oil wash in the winter, with a subsequent spring spray against summer

Free-standing espalier pears in blossom at The Courts, Holt, in Wiltshire, England.

pests (applied walking backwards!) suffices.

The French and Dutch have always been the masters of fruit cultivation in pots. A seventeenth- to nineteenth-century garden would be especially suitable for the gardener with limited space. The kitchen garden has changed so little over the last 200 years, except for the availability of varieties of both fruit and vegetables, that there is little necessity to strive for period accuracy, except to avoid modern plastic-ware, sprays and manufactured fertilizers. The practice of growing trained fruit in

At Westbury Court, Glos., seventeenth-century apple cultivars are trained as wall-grown espaliers.

Training fruit trees

Fruit trees have been trained for centuries for practical reasons as well as decorative: the regular pruning and cutting back encourages a more intensive crop and makes harvesting more manageable. During the nineteenth century the practice developed into something of a mania in Europe and particularly in England, partly due to the upsurge in varieties of fruit trees available. Trees were trained in a wide range of patterns, sometimes covering an entire house front, and designs were even more elaborate in the garden. The most popular shapes, though, have always included espalier, cordon, fan-shaped, and patterns based on the letter 'U' (see below).

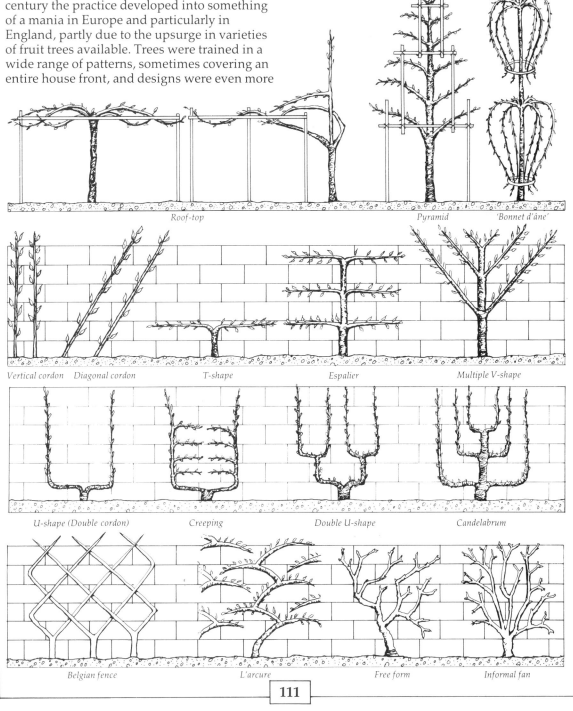

Roof-top *Pyramid* *'Bonnet d'âne'*

Vertical cordon *Diagonal cordon* *T-shape* *Espalier* *Multiple V-shape*

U-shape (Double cordon) *Creeping* *Double U-shape* *Candelabrum*

Belgian fence *L'arcure* *Free form* *Informal fan*

pots is almost a lost skill, and should be undertaken, at first, in quite a limited way.

The root systems of pot-grown fruits are restricted in growth, and are therefore economical to feed. Apples, pears, plums and cherries need pollinators, so select more than one compatible variety – or grow a 'family tree' grafted on to one stock (a modern idea and not for the purist period gardener). Peaches, apricots, nectarines, figs and vines are self-fertilizing, although it is always advisable to hand pollinate from one plant to the next at blossom time to safeguard the harvest. Any pot-grown fruit must not be allowed to overcrop. Plants can be trained as bush, espalier, fan, cordon or pyramid.

The Architectural Fruit Garden

Apples or pears grown as loose cordons on arches over the vegetable pathway would give a nineteenth-century British or eighteenth-century French air to a garden. Supports made from modern durable plastic serve every bit as well as iron ones.

Walls or fences could uphold cordon, or double-cordon apples, espalier pears, fan-trained figs, peaches, nectarines or cherries. For the latter, even north-facing walls in northern Europe (or south-facing ones in Southern Australia and New Zealand) can be used for particular varieties. The old grille-like fruit supports, for forming corridors and screens, can be represented by wires firmly extended from one upright post to the next.

Top fruit can also be trained on a frame, fashioned like a dunce's hat (*bonnet d'âne*).

Fruit Under Glass

In seventeenth-century England, gardeners seem to have expected exotic fruit to ripen in cooler climates simply by the application of heat. On large estates, walls were erected

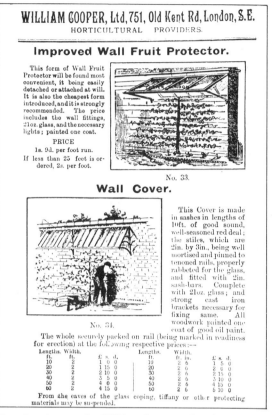

An advertisement for William Cooper's glass fruit protectors, from earlier this century.

to retain the sun's heat; grates, flues and fires were contrived to ward off frost, and hooks high up on the wall provided for drapes to be hung as frost protection. Roller blinds or thin fibre matting were fitted on to these brackets, and later sectional wood framework, covered with thin white cloth or paper both oiled to repel rain and maintain translucence, was used. When glass became cheaper permanent lean-to greenhouses were popular, especially for peach and nectarine cultivation. The retaining wall was almost always painted white to compensate for the loss of light.

All over Europe, except in the very warm countries, purpose-built hot houses were

The charm of this herb garden at Cranbourne, Dorset could be recreated in any kitchen garden today.

constructed. Oranges and lemons, in particular, were cultivated in such houses, known as orangeries or, in France, *citronnières*. Small individual citrus trees were grown in wooden tubs (usually square), which could be transported on trolleys out of doors in the summer. The Dutch took this *Citrus* cultivation method very seriously; one result was that sailors were provided with the fruit to protect them against scurvy.

The first winter shelter was made by Salomon de Caus at Heidelberg in Germany. A type of free-standing, windowless barn, it was erected each winter around and above the trees, and dismantled the following spring. Very soon, it became general practice to transport the plants rather than the building. One of the largest orangeries was built for Louis XIV at Versailles; it housed 1,200 *Citrus* trees and 300 other exotic plants. Braziers, sometimes mobile, provided the heat but, as John Evelyn observed in 1688, 'stoves absolutely destroy our conservatories'.

While few gardeners possess an orangery today, and *Citrus* fruits ripened without intense overhead sunshine lack both aroma and flavour, a porch, conservatory or house extension will provide winter protection. Insufficient winter light is often the cause of failure, but even if the fruit does not form and ripen well, the trim tubs and trees give a period air to the terrace. Lemons grown in tubs require less light than other *Citrus* fruit and are suitable for sheltered districts. Italian gardens abound with pot-grown lemons, although even there they are taken into *serre*, or limoniums, in the coldest periods.

Thinking in Period

The gardener who wishes to recreate a fruit or kitchen garden as accurately as possible will have to accept the old methods of cultivation, *and* use the old materials too. Learn to handle a good pruning knife successfully, instead of using secateurs; use bast or raffia for tying back fruit trees instead of plastic ties; avoid nylon netting; use clay pots; revert to chicken wire, and remember that the hose that carries water under pressure was not invented until the middle of the nineteenth century.

A sixteenth-century Persian miniature of pavilion and pool.

7

WATER IN THE GARDEN

W ater is much more than just a utilitarian element: it has a fascination that sometimes reaches the point of a spiritual craving. Lake, sea or river has an almost irresistible pull, and springs have always been invested with magic origins. Some of the most extraordinary sights in the world are dominated by great rivers, or cascades falling in giant waterfalls from mountainsides. Water has a compelling power over the imagination: many gardens are founded on it, rather than on trees and flowers.

From about the eleventh century, in the earliest Persian gardens – the influence of which spread through the Mogul gardens of northern India and through North Africa to Spain, and then northwards again – water was an essential feature. It was necessary to conserve water in tanks in order to grow trees for shade and the scented plants – Jasmine in particular – that were vital to the notion of paradise. Paradise itself has four rivers, and courtyards or gardens were divided into four symbolic segments, a water tank fed by a fountain being set in the centre. This was the style of the patio later adopted in Spain, around the thirteenth century. It has in turn been used in every country where buildings are constructed round a square. The Spanish patio, but equally the historic gardens of Spain, offers a model for small gardens of today.

Water Tanks

The tank is the easiest kind of pool to install and offers an excellent view of any plants and fish: they are closer to eye level than when the pool is set in the ground. No excavation is needed; the square or oblong fibreglass container bought from a garden centre is simply set on a level base. Alternatively, a discarded water cistern can be used. A more ambitious plan is to use an octagon, following the pattern of the pools seen in paintings of old Persian gardens. The early designers, preoccupied with geometry, laid one square within another to produce this form. The walls should be made of concrete or breeze blocks laid on edge in either one or two courses, the whole then given a sand base and lined with stout polythene, or, better still, with butyl rubber sheeting sold for making garden pools.

The sides should be faced either with exposed aggregate paving slabs or with ceramic tiles laid to a Moorish pattern. A coping stone should be laid at the top, flat and wide enough to take the weight of a person or, at least, a series of decorative terracotta or glazed pots, all of the same size and pattern, and planted identically for the summer months.

Water Channels

One of the traditions of the Muslim garden was that the pool should always be brimming with constantly refreshed water, the overflow being conducted through narrow channels which became part of the design. This idea was embraced by European gardeners. In the garden of Hestercombe, in Somerset, rills, as the channels came to be called in this context, take the overflow from wall fountains that play into basins set in a massive retaining wall. They each run centrally through a panel of turf towards an outlet and become an interesting garden feature, especially in the way that, at intervals, their line is broken by a circle of stone to provide an individual bed for a moisture-loving iris and the dramatic outline made by its sword-like foliage.

The public gardens in Hamburg include a small garden laid out with paving stones outlined with water in the same way as they are sometimes surrounded by a line of brick. Half-round tiles are laid on a bed of cement, necessarily with a very slight tilt to one lower point; this can be made by shaping narrow strips of polythene.

A Spanish-style pool with Moorish tiles.

A slim channel of water was a feature of Italian Renaissance gardens, this time running downhill, where it became a water staircase, eddying through a series of basins to divert its flow, the channel either flanking a long flight of steps or bisecting it, as at the garden of the Villa Lante at Bagnaia, built in the sixteenth century. An earlier example is in the thirteenth century Generalife gardens at Granada in Spain, where the balustrades beside several flights of steps are capped with half-round tiles through which the water runs.

The water parterre to which the flow

The sunken garden, Hestercombe, Somerset.

descends through several complexes of fountains has been adopted effectively by the international landscape architect Russell Page in a contemporary garden in the south of France, where box-edged beds of white flowers – pansies for winter and spring, petunias for summer – alternate with rectangular pools of equal size within the overall scheme. Rectangular pools are easy to create with polythene or rubber sheeting, and the idea has many possibilities for small gardens, providing a sense of spaciousness within a mannered style.

Fountains

Many of the patio pools in Spanish gardens are like shallow basins, either saucer-shaped or scalloped to form a stylized lotus-like outline. These are to be seen both at the Generalife and the Alhambra. There are many modern reproductions available, and water garden specialists often stock such pools, either in reconstituted stone or terracotta. Generally, they are fashioned to be fed by fountains in the classical manner,

The water parterre at Castel Montegues by Russell Page.

although the water is propelled by a small electric pump instead of coming from a natural spring.

One especially fine modern garden, which employs many 'classical' fountains, does use an ever-running flow of water from natural sources – from higher on the hillsides on which its terraces lie. This is the Villa Noailles, at Grasse, in the south of France, begun in the 1930s and developed

A peaceful corner at Villa Noailles.

The outlines of these pools are softened by plantings.

A Persian Garden

A national style of gardening is determined by the country's natural resources and climate. In the arid lands of Persia, water played an important role in garden design because it was an essential. Irrigation canals gave the garden its traditional square or rectilinear form and enclosing walls protected it from drying winds. Thus far it is a clear case of form following function, and although irrigation may hardly be a necessity in Northern Europe the plan is simple enough to adapt.

In a Persian garden water should be treated with sophisticated restraint; do not crowd it with statuary or contort it into high jet fountains. The effect to aim for is not grandiose but serene; the beauty of water must be allowed to speak for itself, to flow in long rills or wide canals, rest reflective in still pools of clean geometric outline or burble into a simple 'bubble-jet' fountain.

The Persians used glazed tiles to edge their pools and canals but these would be unsuitable in a European garden unless in a frost-free area. Quarry tiles of hexagonal or octagonal shape would be a practical alternative and could be carried through as a paving material.

Symbolically, the Persian paradise garden contained all the fruits and flowers of the earth. Avenues of tall cypresses represented death and eternity, and flowering fruit trees life and fertility. The Italian Cypress (*Cupressus sempervirens*) may not be reliably hardy in all areas but the Irish fastigiate Yew (*Taxus baccata fastigiata*) makes an adequate substitute. Blossoming trees (almond, cherry, apricot and peach), essential to the character of a Persian garden, should be grown as espaliers around the perimeter wall, with Day lilies (*Hemerocallis flava* and *H. fulva*) at their feet. Tulips, pinks and irises would also be appropriate, but the rose was esteemed above every other flower; the species they grew were the ancient shrub roses, *R. damascena*, *R. gallica* and the hardy *R. rugosa*.

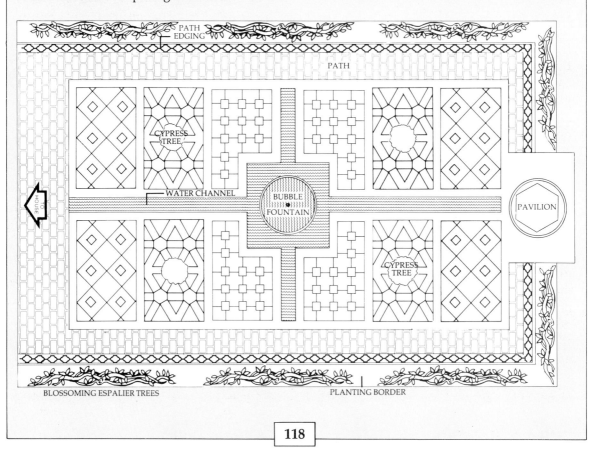

BLOSSOMING ESPALIER TREES — PLANTING BORDER

in the late 1940s, which places many historical garden features within a contemporary setting.

As a garden feature the fountain owes its origins to the classical gardens created by the Romans. The younger Pliny described in detail the contrived waterworks of his own hillside garden in Tuscany, and from him the Renaissance architect Leone Battista Alberti took the ideas he codified in a famous treatise that influenced Italian garden making as a whole. Alberti specified that gardens should be made on hillsides for refreshment and delight – and running water was an essential ingredient.

Fountains were constructed in most Renaissance gardens. The most elaborate constructions were at the Villa d'Este at Tivoli, an area famous for its retreat gardens. Its moss-encrusted Terrace of a Hundred Fountains provided inspiration for a tufa-faced wall at the Villa Noailles. There, a short retaining wall about 30 m (100 feet) high is faced with tufa rock through which the water tumbles into a trough, then continues to feed other fountains. The great water organ of the Villa d'Este, a vast assembly of jets which pass through many devices to produce startling musical sounds, is equally famous. The idea has its modern counterpart in an English garden in Dorset made by Sir Geoffrey Jellicoe, where, as the water passes from pool to pool, each on a lower level, through copper pipes of different sizes, it sounds a chord. The rectangular pools, although surrounded by rich plantings, are gardens in themselves, and well illustrate the essential point that formal water gardens of geometric outlines are more suitable for a limited site than an informal feature inspired by natural lakes.

While the great Renaissance gardens, alive with fountains, channelled their wa-

The late Sir William Walton's high-jet fountain at Ischia.

ter from natural springs employing the techniques the Romans used for their aqueducts, the water gardens they inspired usually relied on the hydraulic water pump. The most striking, and absurd, example is at Versailles. To feed the fountains and the 1.6-km (1-mile) long canal, streams had to be diverted, and since all the fountains could not play simultaneously, when Louis XIV went on his progress around the garden attended by a great retinue of courtiers, workmen had to be on hand to turn on various taps at his approach and increase the pressure by closing others.

Nowadays, a small electric pump, cheap to buy and easy to install, can propel a garden fountain, even high jets like those in the nineteenth-century Derbyshire garden at Chatsworth and in Lake Leman at Geneva, or the more recently constructed ravine garden made for the composer Sir William Walton on the island of Ischia in the Bay of Naples. In each case, the water is circulated; it requires no natural source, and the pool need only be topped up as the water is lost by evaporation. Tall single jets, however, can be a hazard on windy days; it is better to settle for a low multi-jet fountain that the breeze cannot take very far. The basin into which it plays can be a decorative feature, not only in outline but also in its lining, which can consist of tiles or mosaic laid to a pattern. The tiles or mosaic can simply be stuck to the liner with waterproof adhesive.

A bubble fountain, whose jet rises only a few centimetres with the water tumbling back into a shallow basin or over some carved or natural blocks of stone, can introduce the perennially fascinating element of moving water. These can easily be constructed by casting an object in tinted cement, and passing a length of the copper piping used in domestic central heating through the centre to take the water. It is possible to buy traditional figures reproduced from classical models, which lend themselves to a bubbling jet as much as to a soaring fountain.

In some of the most celebrated water gardens in history – those of the Moguls in India, for example – what today are small fountains were originally no more than jets giving little plumes of water rising from geometric pools. The purpose of the niches at the sides of the pools was for inserting lamps at night: if the simplest garden can be fitted with an electric pump for a jet, waterfall or fountain, it can also have the added refinement of lighting to bring a theatrical sense to the scheme and enable it to be enjoyed after dark.

Cascades and Waterfalls

The cascade, in which water tumbles down a hillside in a series of waterfalls channelled within formally constructed bounds, is a familiar feature of Italian gardens, not-

A decorative pebble pattern lines this placid pool.

ably at the sixteenth-century Villa Aldobrandini at Frascati. After leaving its grotto high on the hill, the water sparkles down twin pillars of helter-skelter design, and then takes a course over a series of broad steps. Always in a formal setting, such a cascade makes a great sound of rushing water. It can be adapted to a sloping site of any size, using pumping equipment.

It is simpler to make a waterfall from a stream (using pumps again) which runs through a miniature ravine and tumbles into a small informal pool surrounded by rocks. Such a scheme is in character, however, only where the site has a steep slope and where the informal garden is successfully integrated into its immediate environment.

Swimming Pools

How far swimming pools and even children's paddling pools can be integrated into a period garden depends on the amount of room available, either for giving it an enclosure of its own or for accom-

A 'Japanese corner' made with water, bamboo and stone.

Terracotta oil jars make an enchanting fountain head.

A wall-mounted fountain is one of the simplest ways to introduce water to the period garden.

panying it by other pools that are purely decorative – a device which has been used very successfully in some contemporary gardens.

The circular carp pool in the early twentieth-century Hidcote garden in Gloucestershire was once the bathing pool of the property. It lies within its own hedged enclosure, surrounded by richly planted flower-beds of shrubs and herbaceous perennials, with bulbs for spring effect.

The original owner also created a garden in the south of France, the legendary Serre de la Madonne, where he made a rectangular bathing pool, integrating it into the scheme of the garden by setting another pool at one end, this time crescent-shaped, which was planted with lotus. At regular intervals along the coping stones of the bathing pool stood giant glazed terracotta vases, each with its standard trained citrus tree. The same device was used in the Villa Taranto garden on Lake Maggiore, which was begun in the early 1930s; here, the whole was partly enclosed by a pergola.

Children's plastic pools can be surrounded with brick, concrete or breeze-block low walling, and then clad with tiles or mosaic to make them resemble the tank-like pools of the Moorish gardens in Spain.

A Simple, Decorative Waterflow

One of the simplest ways of introducing water to the period garden is to run a pipe through one of the joints in a brick or stone retaining wall and allow the water to gush from a decorative mask cemented to the wall into a tank or trough. A discarded fire-clay sink can be used effectively if the glaze is chipped with a cold chisel and then the surface coated with cement that has been mixed with peat. The result is to make it appear like old stone. A circulating electric pump could be used, and the trough will also serve as a dipping-well on occasions for garden watering.

The Informal Pool

The informal pool owes its introduction to the garden to the great eighteenth-century landscapes, from which formality was banished and at which time a premium was placed upon the simplicity and irregularity of nature. It reached its highest horticultural point when the water was surrounded by plantings of the new hardy primulas brought in from the great Asiatic plant collecting expeditions, and with the native ferns discovered in the wild by amateur botanists in the first quarter of the present century. From there it has gone on to become a small garden feature, thanks to the introduction of simple plastic pool liners for installing in small gardens that echo nature rather than architecture, and represent an idealized version of a natural scene.

As these liners are never fitted with

The delightful rock garden pool at Sizergh Castle.

drainage plugs and therefore overflow in periods of heavy rain, the surrounding ground which becomes flooded can be put to use as bog garden. To provide for spells when the ground would dry out it is wise to install a layer of stout polythene – pierced here and there with a garden fork – 45 centimetres (18 inches) below the surface, to help retain the moisture in the upper soil level.

Though the plastic liners are of irregular outline, it is important to set them level in a bed of dry sand so that the water reaches the rim all the way round. Use a board placed from edge to edge and a spirit level to check. Another useful tip is to paint them black with bitumen paint rather than leave them in their own green or pale blue plastic colouring. This gives a more natural appearance and makes them seem deeper. Where the site is on a slope a series of such pools can be installed, waterfalls linking them. In fact, sets of liners are sold with outlets for this purpose. An electric pump circulates the water back to the top pool.

8
GATES, WALLS AND BOUNDARIES

Illustrations of medieval and Renaissance gardens invariably show a perimeter security wall: its vulnerable point was the place of entry, and the gates were likely to be sturdily made from solid oak with some iron reinforcement. They were little different from the external doors to the house. The oak gate was left untreated and with the passage of time developed a silvery colouring.

By the more peaceful seventeenth century the openwork gate made of wrought iron replaced the solid door. It gave inviting views into the gardens, while at the same time barring unwelcome guests. The entrance no longer had to be an opening in the wall: instead the wall was lower and stopped on both sides of the gate. The ends of the two walls were finished with decorative piers supporting the gate.

These piers had some distinguishing treatments, especially in the seventeenth century, such as string courses, cornices and copings topped with large stone finials. More important gate piers would incorporate niches in the outer face. In towns, however, where more security was required, arched or lintel-formed openings into higher walls continued to be employed for garden entrances. If the opening was an archway, the areas between the arch and the top of the gate could be filled in with an overthrow of ironwork.

Before the seventeenth century – except when working for the grandest establishments – ironsmiths had largely concentrated on making utilitarian products for the community. But with artist/craftsmen such as Jean Tijou, a Huguenot refugee who came to Britain in 1689, the highest achievements of the blacksmith's craft became associated with gates, piers and screens made for important gardens. Tijou's gates and screens along a part of the river frontage of the gardens at Hampton Court Palace, near London, can still be seen and admired today.

By the eighteenth century, wrought iron had become the usual material for gates to most gardens, except in some areas such as

Seventeenth-century garden doorway made of solid oak at Packwood House, Warwickshire.

Wrought iron gate in seventeenth-century brickwork, with recesses for bee skips. Packwood House, Warwicks.

the United States of America, where gates and fences were still made in timber but with open latticework in the upper parts of the gate. For important gardens and college grounds, the ironwork might include monograms and heraldry.

But whether the grandest or the simplest wrought iron gate, a basic pattern was followed. Stouter members formed the gate frame which was filled with vertical bars, the tops of which could have finials in the form of arrows or spearheads – meant as a deterrent to intruders. The lower part of the gate had a row of intermediate bars known as dog bars; their purpose was to keep out dogs and other small animals. For the more elaborate gates, the finials were sometimes replaced by an overthrow of ironwork, incorporating motifs worked in sheet metal and elegant scrolls. The overthrow usually built up to its highest point in the middle and was made either as part of the gate

itself or fixed independently above it between the gate piers.

If you are fortunate enough to obtain a genuine wrought iron gate, it must be sited carefully in a position that is in scale with it. To ensure that rusting does not develop it should be painted regularly and any restoration work carried out by experienced craftsmen.

Wrought iron is still occasionally used by craftsmen, but, more commonly, reproductions are manufactured in wrought steel, protected by galvanizing and regular painting. The cheap designs with their feeble curved decoration will instantly kill any period feeling in a garden. It is possible to find hand made gates in steel which closely resemble simple wrought iron examples; however, they are more expensive, and if you have one made you must give adequate instructions about the sort of design you want.

Timber gate with attractive latticework.

Wrought iron gate , shown off by the wall beyond.

In the nineteenth century, some cast iron gates were made for gardens. These gates frequently used an overall design motif in place of the vertical bars. Cast iron gates are heavier looking and not usually as elegant as those made in wrought iron. In addition, the material is more brittle, making it less hardwearing.

Iron gates should be painted black or ordnance blue (a dark blue/black colour); however, if they are viewed against a dark background, such as a yew hedge, white is better, providing it will not look too harsh. Decorative items in the gate, such as finials and monograms, may be picked out in gold leaf and any heraldry painted in true heraldic colours. Never be tempted to use gold substitutes because, out-of-doors, they will quickly tarnish to a disappointing khaki.

Wrought iron gates, whether new or re-used old ones, remained popular until the Second World War, and, consequently, they are not out of date in any garden from the seventeenth century onwards. However, from the late nineteenth century until about the 1940s, many garden designers favoured ornamental garden gates constructed in timber. The designs were architectural in flavour and the gates well constructed. It is only too easy to ruin a period garden with an off-the-shelf gate, but many magazines and books published during the 1920s and 1930s show good designs to copy for timber gates. They should be made from hardwood, preferably oak, and constructed to the best traditional standards for out-of-doors joinery. Oak left untreated will weather to a fine light silvery colour, which looks marvellous next to mellow old stonework. However, at the time many were painted white, sometimes to tie in with a scheme of white timber features in the garden.

Walls

Throughout history, walls have served a variety of important functions. Along with gates they afford enclosure and security to the garden and house. A wall also changes the local climate, giving the garden shelter as well as acting as a sun trap. A southerly facing wall (or, in the Southern Hemisphere, a northern one) encourages plants and fruit which, if in the open, would be difficult to grow. The training of fruit trees to grow on sunny walls has been practised for centuries, before glasshouses were used. Many old garden walls still have hot-air flues to prevent late spring frosts damaging the flowers and setting fruit. With the terracing of sloping ground, from the Renaissance onwards, it became necessary to build retaining walls, most of which also had a parapet wall, usually ornamental. Walls were also used in gardens to mask unsightly areas such as kitchen courtyards.

Well proportioned stone balustrading with carved pier and ball finial at St. Catherine's Court, near Bath.

Arbours and Pergolas

Arbours and pergolas were popular during the nineteenth and twentieth centuries, and they will provide an authentic feature for your period garden.

After the sprawling landscapes of the eighteenth century, the Victorians made a return to formality in the garden. Industrialization brought about an increase in urban living; gardens were subsequently smaller and designed for family use once more. The Victorian mania for decoration is apparent in the delicate wirework arbours popular during the period. Reproductions of these, and matching garden furniture, are manufactured today. Although they are generally painted white, a dark green or brown would be more appropriate to a nineteenth-century garden. Set on a smooth green lawn and planted with roses such as 'Gloire de Dijon' or 'Madame Alfred Carrière', a wirework arbour would instantly summon a Victorian ambience.

By the end of the nineteenth

A Victorian wirework arbour

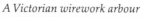

Most garden walls were built in either stone or brick, according to availability. Although the local resources may have changed since a house and garden were built, it is desirable to maintain the continuity of materials for new garden work, especially close to the house.

Straight walls can be built with greater economy if piers are constructed at regular intervals. The serpentine wall, in fact, evolved from the need to economize: built in East Anglia at least from the eighteenth century, it was copied by Thomas Jefferson at the University of Virginia. In addition to its strength and economy of materials, the concave aspects on the side of the wall facing the sun are ideal for growing certain plants and fruits.

The type of walling needing most detailed historical accuracy is the retaining wall with its parapet. (The purpose of the parapet is to prevent people from falling off

Stone retaining wall and decorative parapet in the garden at St. Catherine's Court, near Bath.

century and in the beginning of the twentieth century the 'wild' garden became popular, and in accordance with this arbours and pergolas were made of rustic wood (branches with the bark left on). Although the life expectancy of this material is not very long it is a relatively inexpensive way of recreating a period feature. Planting should be generous – perhaps a combination of Penzance sweet briars and clematis.

The masters of garden design in the opening decades of this century were primarily architects. Pergolas made of vernacular materials, such as stone, tile or brick, with heavy oak cross beams, were frequently an important element in the garden. The emphasis was on solidity and craftsmanship. Well made hardwood furniture would complement the scene and pillar roses, vines and wisteria would be a good selection of plants.

A rustic pergola

the retaining wall.) In the garden, the wall is invariably made into a decorative feature, with balustrading and piers at intervals. The balustrades reflect every architectural and gardening style; it is most important to use a style which suits any adjoining house or garden building, as well as the period garden itself.

In the early decades of this century it was common in stony regions to build retaining walls in gardens to provide a home for wall-loving rockery plants. Pockets of soil would be left for their planting, or, in the case of dry stone walling, space was allowed for the roots to penetrate to the retained soil.

Walls constructed from local materials have, over the centuries, produced distinct and characteristic vernacular styles that transcend historical ones. A designer working in a rural area will normally wish to work within local tradition, using the available stone and prevailing techniques for wall construction.

New walls or repairs to existing ones will look more in character if the mortar joints are raked out, allowing the stone or brick to be emphasized. Care must be taken to choose suitable mortars both for strength and appearance: try to find types which give a softer, mellower tone than is common nowadays. Local craftsmen and designers will give invaluable advice on the best choice of ingredients and mix for a particular wall.

Clair-voyées

Walls enclosing small and even medium-sized gardens in flat topography give an introverted mood to the garden. This enclosed feeling was not always desirable, and the *clair-voyée* was a means of reducing the effect. Much used in French and Dutch gardens and introduced to Britain during the reign of William and Mary, it consisted of open panels of wrought ironwork, which could be set into an opening in the wall, or supported between piers. Designed to give security without obscuring the view, these garden windows would normally be placed at the end of vistas in the formal garden of the seventeenth century and remained in favour until the landscape style of gardening became

Plants and fruit grow well against this eighteenth-century serpentine wall at Heveningham Hall, Suffolk.

The ha-ha was used in eighteenth-century landscape gardens to keep animals away from the house and lawns.

fashionable. If the view from the garden could also be to something of landscape interest, such as a river with its constantly moving traffic, so much the better.

The Ha-ha

The natural progression from the *clair-voyée* was to the ha-ha, or sunken wall, which allowed a completely uninterrupted view of the more natural world beyond the garden. The ha-ha seems to have its origins in the outer trench of Renaissance military defences. It was incorporated into the evolving landscape garden early in the eighteenth century. By the 1760s it was widely used to keep the grazing animals of the landscape park away from the house and its surrounding lawns and gardens.

The ha-ha is formed by excavating a deep ditch which, on the house side, is given a masonry retaining wall to a height sufficient to stop animals climbing over it, and, on the park side, a sloping profile which prohibits the animals leaping over both the ditch and wall. To the eye, viewed from the house and garden, the continuity of grass from lawn to pasture is surprisingly effective; the ha-ha is only discovered when one is almost upon it.

The ha-ha is still used today; for example, in a small garden bordering a field of sheep. The height of the retaining wall will depend on the type of animals to be kept out – obviously, for sheep the height will be less than for red deer. Comparable ha-has still in effective use should be examined before deciding on all the dimensions. (Beware of old ha-has, some of which are filled up with leaf mould and trampled-down soil.)

Iron Railings and Fencing

From the eighteenth century onwards, decorative iron railings have been a common means of enclosing gardens, especially around the forecourts of houses. The railings consist of vertical rods capped with pointed finials representing arrowheads, spears and fleurs-de-lis, fixed into a low wall and held together at the top by a horizontal bar. At intervals, further strengthening is provided by masonry or iron piers. Piers, corner posts and gate posts in iron have a larger finial of cast iron with urns, acorns and pine cones being the favourite motifs. Originally, railings were made of wrought iron, but the cheaper cast iron was soon more popular.

In the nineteenth century, many parks were enclosed by long stretches of iron fencing made up of several horizontal flat bars, which were supported by uprights at regular intervals. The uprights had a forked end for fixing into the ground, and the whole fence was continuous for more stability. Intended to contain livestock, a taller version of this straightforward fencing was used, especially in deer parks, where it would also protect plantations within the park. It was made of wrought iron and, because of its considerable resistance to anything more than surface rusting, has lasted extremely well.

Cast iron railings can be re-cast at an iron foundry (a single bar will suffice as a model). Wrought iron is much less easily available today, and copies will probably have to be made in galvanized steel and then painted. Many modern steel railings only mimic, rather than reproduce, the qualities of the old railings.

Timber Fences

In pre-eighteenth-century gardens, timber was usually used for fencing which attached deer parks and gardens to small properties. For cottages, the most appropriate is a palisade fence, consisting of vertical pickets attached to two horizontal members and supported just above the ground by hardwood posts or piers. This type of fencing was made from wrought timber and painted white. The tops of the pickets were given a pointed end which could be made a little more elaborate for decorative effect. Country railway station fencing is in this style; the tradition for using this fencing remains strong in the eastern United States of America.

A more rustic type of timber fence associated with some estate cottages is made from cleft poles nailed to horizontal members in a criss-cross pattern, and left unpainted. Sweet chestnut and ash from coppiced woods are usually used for these fences.

Trellis-work

Trellis-work is a very old form of garden ornament; there is pictorial evidence of it being used in ancient Chinese and Roman gardens. It probably originated as a support for climbing plants, but soon combined plant support with decorative screening. In the seventeenth and eighteenth centuries, trellises were worked into architectural forms such as temples and various *trompe l'oeil* devices, where the false perspective deceived the eye into thinking that a design was three-dimensional when, in fact, it was flat.

In medieval and Renaissance gardens,

Nineteenth-century Fence and Gate Patterns

A fence is ideal for delineating a border without losing light or creating a hemmed-in feeling. Rather than buying an 'off-the shelf' design, make or have made a fence or gate that will be in keeping with the period of your house and garden. A good public library should be able to provide plenty of source material from which you can copy or adapt period designs, or you can have sections of an existing item copied.

The designs shown here are from a German magazine of 1810. Throughout the nineteenth century the most popular materials for fences and gates were wrought iron, cast iron and rustic timber.

A wrought-iron fence would be most appropriate in the front garden of a formal house, but if it is put straight into the ground it will quickly rust away. To prevent this, and to increase the strength and stability of the wrought iron, it must be used in association with a low stone or brick wall.

Cast iron was mass produced in the nineteenth century and was widely used for balconies and conservatories. Its fluid shapes associate well with plants but it is very heavy; care must be taken with its fixing, and it should be treated for rust. Painted white it would make a delightful railing for a roof garden or a patio. Cast-iron railings can be bought second-hand, and only one section is

needed for a foundry to cast as much as is necessary.

Timber is still the most frequently used fencing material because of its flexibility and economy. With imaginative treatment and a little extra care it should be possible to design and construct a fence or gate of

unique but appropriate style, using rustic timber or even working within the confines of standardized timber sizing. Try to avoid choosing the most obvious design for your gate or fence – an unusual design is not necessarily complex and will add style to your garden.

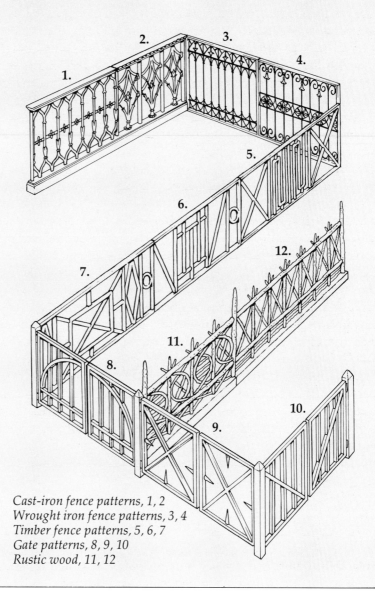

Cast-iron fence patterns, 1, 2
Wrought iron fence patterns, 3, 4
Timber fence patterns, 5, 6, 7
Gate patterns, 8, 9, 10
Rustic wood, 11, 12

trellis-work formed cloistered walks around small gardens with domes as arbours over seats. Sometimes called timber galleries, they were constructed in fairly substantial latticework of oak and oak framework. The reconstructed Elizabethan knot garden at New Place, Stratford-upon-Avon, has a good example of such a timber gallery supporting trained fruit trees.

In France, from the seventeenth century, the design of trellis-work became a notable part of garden design. Very elaborate structures were created, both free standing and for wall decoration, and the art continues to remain popular there today.

A number of designs for ambitious trellis-work constructions were published in France and in Britain during the eighteenth century. The designs were usually planned to close vistas or to form an enclosed end to a garden scene.

For town gardens, trellis-work has been well utilized this century; it is used in conservatories and even in restaurants. For small spaces, it can create interest, surprise and illusions in areas which might otherwise be dark and dull.

Although various materials have been used, laths supported on a timber framework is the most popular construction.

Timber trellis-work can be used to great effect in a small town garden. Here seen at Bodnant, North Wales.

Metal, in the form of an iron framework with infilling of wirework lattice, was popular for Victorian arbours, and a number of examples have survived. Today, a ready-made standard criss-cross trellis, which can form the basis for screens and more elaborate constructions, is available. Laths are often made from Western red cedar and are joined together by non-ferrous nails.

9

PATHS
AND STEPS

T here are three basic categories of path: hard paths of brick, tiles, or of natural stones and pebbles; flexible paths of gravel, sand or ashes; and soft paths of grass or creeping plants. All have a place in the period garden, although a successful path, which takes a lot of wear from foot traffic and wheelbarrows, must be well constructed. It is better to use a less expensive material and do a thorough job than to try a more ambitious scheme which you cannot afford to carry out properly.

Hard Paths
Artificially made materials

BRICK

Paths made of brick are beautiful, but some can be treacherously slippery in wet weather. Many bricks are not weather-proof, so in areas which become frosty the bricks must be extremely hard to withstand the combined effects of wet and cold. Especially hard bricks, known as paviors, are made for the purpose, and in some areas bricks which have become over-heated and mis-shapen in the kiln – often called 'overbakes' – are obtainable quite cheaply and are excellent for informal and rustic effects.

The bricks can either be laid flat or on edge; the latter method practically doubles the number required to cover an area, but gives a much finer texture to the finished work. The most familiar pattern for laying, the herringbone, is one of the most difficult to carry out well and requires skilful cutting and fitting at the edges. Much easier are the various forms of basket-weave, in which the bricks are laid in alternating squares. It is best to try laying out sample panels, seeing which pattern is most pleasing and best fitted for the scale of the path which you propose to build.

A base of concrete should be laid first, and then with a true surface to work on the subsequent laying is quite quick. Alternatively, on firm, well-consolidated soils, lay 7.5 cm (3 inches) of firmed and levelled sand, then lay the bricks packed with more sand. The bricks are better dampened before use, and then spread with a little

A good example of a herringbone brick path. Though difficult to achieve, the effect is very pleasing.

thin mortar on the back. They should be tapped into position with the wooden handle of a plasterer's trowel. It is not essential to point between the joints – which allow good drainage and the planting of small creeping plants such as thyme – but pointing looks neater, is stronger, and prevents weed growth. Good pointing can be tinted to suit the colour of the brick and the position of the paths by mixing the cement with different coloured sands. Rub the joints with a rag to give a softer look.

Because of the size of each unit, brick is traditional for small-scale work and is also used in narrow bands to form the pattern in a knot or herb garden. In character, brick belongs to any of the periods of pleasance garden and for small layouts of formal type.

Brick path patterns

Brick paths can be the most beautiful of all, and there are a number of patterns to choose from. Herringbone is one of the most pleasing patterns to look at, but is more difficult to achieve well than the many variations of the basket-weave pattern. Try out sample patterns to see which will be the most suitable for the path you require; and ensure that you use locally made bricks, which will blend in much more effectively with the colours of your garden.

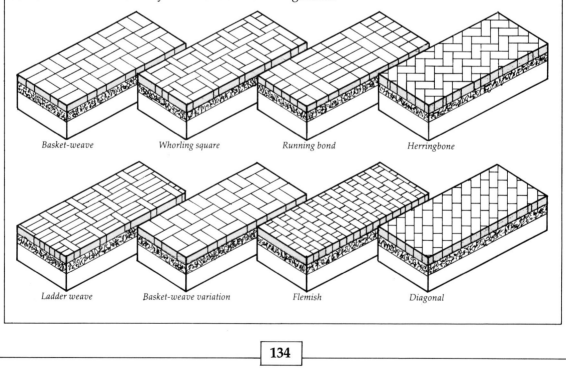

Basket-weave   Whorling square   Running bond   Herringbone

Ladder weave   Basket-weave variation   Flemish   Diagonal

A brick path laid in the basket-weave pattern leads to the White Garden at Sissinghurst Castle.

Roof tiles laid flat over a concrete base make an attractive surface. Here the holes for the nails add interest.

TILE

Sometimes it is possible to retrieve old square tiles from a demolished kitchen or dairy and these can make beautiful paths, laid in the same way as bricks. In the nineteenth-century garden, roof tiles were occasionally used on edge to create interesting sunburst patterns of radiating lines. These are effective in emphasizing an ornament or making a central feature in a brick or stone-paved court. However, the work needs to be very well done and it is not easy to get regular lines given the small size of a tile, so experiment before starting. Roof tiles of suitable shape can also be laid flat over a concrete base (first dipped in water and then bedded down into a thin mixture of cement and sand) to produce an effective path which looks well in a cottage-style garden. Each tile should be butted up tightly against its neighbour to avoid the necessity of pointing. Old tiles, perhaps not good enough to be re-used for roofing, might be obtained quite cheaply and would give a very mellow effect.

PRE-CAST SLABS

Nowadays it is possible to obtain a great number of varieties of pre-cast slab, all based on concrete in some form, in a medley of colours which have little place in the reconstruction of a period garden. The one exception is in the Art Deco garden of the 1920s, where square, light-coloured concrete slabs, all the same size, were used with wide joints pointed with a darker cement. Although a very simple treatment, it has to be done perfectly: its purpose was to emphasize slick, machine-made regularity.

The only other slabs appropriate for a period garden are the rather expensive varieties made from crushed, reconstituted stone, which can be used in exactly the same way as real stone slabs. They are easier to lay, but it is important to arrange them in a natural way. One problem is that there are only a limited number of sizes, whereas real slabs have more variation, and it is very easy to slip into laying out a repetitive pattern. If you study an area of stone flag-paving laid in what is called 'random rectangular' fashion, you will see that there is an overall balance between large, intermediate and small stones, but that no pattern or regularity is visible. Slabs should be at least 5 cm (2 inches) thick. Joints must be reasonably wide, as close-butted artificial slabs often look no better than a layer of *in situ* concrete from a short distance away. To give a period effect to a path the pointing should be raked out in the same way as in walls. To do this, fill the joints with cement and then rub the surface with a rag on the end of a stick. Then brush the edges clean with a soft brush. The cement could also be tinted with colour to give a softer, older effect.

When well laid and weathered, reconstituted stone slabs can be very effective. Because of their even thickness they can be laid over a concrete raft in the same way as bricks.

Contemporary diamond-pattern tiles blend surprisingly well into this period environment at Beaulieu.

Path patterns

Considerable charm and character can be added to any path by working in a pattern. Pebble mosaics, common in seventeenth- and eighteenth-century gardens, are very laborious to do except over a small area. In the nineteenth century, roof tiles were sometimes used on edge to create sunburst patterns. Later, there was a fashion for crazy paving and for complex architectural patterns made from stone, brick and tile. Combinations of different materials can create an interesting and characterful effect.

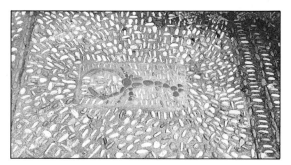

Precast slabs are easy to lay because of their even sizing, and add a formal air.

Natural materials

STONE

Types of stone available vary from area to area within a country, depending on the geological formations and the prevalence of quarries. However, if the stone is to be used for paving, it is essential to choose a variety which is hard-wearing and will stand constant exposure to the weather. If more than one type of stone is used in the same path it is also essential to know that all will wear equally well, otherwise the path may be a patchwork of puddles after rain because some stones were softer than others.

Usually stone flags are laid in the random rectangular manner over a base of hardcore or broken stone. Because the stone slabs are often slightly irregular in thickness, the base should be covered with a layer of sand and each slab set down on five dabs of cement to keep it in place on

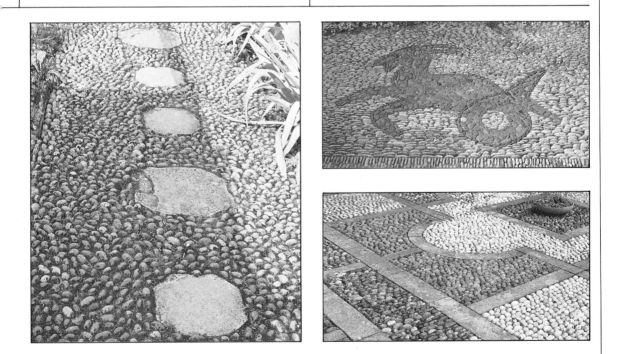

Random rectangular stone flags make a timeless path at St. Catherine's Court near Bath.

the sand bed; the thicker stones can be bedded more deeply than the others. Again, it is important to rake out the pointing, which should be carefully tinted to blend with the colouring of the stone.

In the Arts and Crafts garden of the late nineteenth and early twentieth centuries, paving reached new heights of elaboration. Stone was frequently combined with brick and tile to form complex architectural patterns. Alternatively, a rustic air was given by the use of crazy paving – irregularly shaped pieces of stone fitted together like a jigsaw puzzle, with earth-filled joints in which grew dwarf creeping plants. This form of paving became a great cliché and was seen in many gardens made in the first half of this century. It would lend an authentic period touch to a reconstruction of that time, but the effect is fussy, and if

Shadows accentuate the relief pattern of this cobblestone path.

planted joints are used, maintenance is difficult; it should only be used in moderation and with care.

GRANITE SETTS

These were not normally used for paths since they are uncomfortable to walk on (although easier than cobbles), but they are ideal for courtyards in period surroundings. Each area has traditional patterns and ways of laying setts and it is important to study these and use an appropriate form. Unfortunately new setts are rather expensive and old ones both difficult to find and to use; a great depth of stone is below ground, so that they require a lot of excavation and are heavy to handle. However, excellent reproductions are available, which are reasonable in price and easy to lay.

Whatever surface is used it is essential to have really solid foundations – possibly a slab of reinforced concrete – below any area to be used by wheeled traffic.

COBBLES AND PEBBLES

Cobbles – natural round stones from a beach or stream bed – have the form of an outsize, flattened egg. They are generally used set on end or sometimes, in the case of large ones, on edge to give variation in pattern. Difficult to walk on, they were seldom used for paths but frequently formed part of a design incorporating brick or stone to give a change of texture. They were also used for small-scale features, such as the gutters carrying drainage water at the side of a path or drive, the infill between house wall and path, a circle surrounding a garden ornament or the floor of

Crazy paving creates a rustic air, making it suitable for a cottage garden.

a grotto or summerhouse.

The best way to lay cobbles – a tedious process – is to put down a bed of well-mixed dry sand and cement over a hard-core base, and tap each stone into it with a wooden mallet. When all the stones are level, brush away any loose sand and cement, then gently flood the area with water and leave the cement to set. It is very difficult to get cement off the surface of cobbles once it has dried, so attempting to lay the cobbles in a wet mix generally leads to disaster.

An even more time-consuming variant is pebble paving, in which small rounded pebbles in various colours – grey, black, white, brown, red – are worked into elaborate designs. This technique came from the southern European countries –

Decorative pebble paving is extended to the walls of the garden in the Villa Medici, Italy.

Spain, Italy, Portugal – where there is no frost to disturb the slight hold the pebbles have on their base. Such paths are to be found largely in seventeenth- and eighteenth-century gardens. The motifs employed in the pattern vary with the period, but often include armorial bearings and baroque scrolls, or simpler geometric arrangements. They date from a period when labour was cheap and they are difficult now even to repair, let alone to create afresh. However, a determined garden owner might use pebble paving very effectively over a small area.

STONE PITCHING AND SPALLS

There are other techniques much akin to laying cobbles. For pitching, small stones are set on edge or, if they are spalls, driven pointed end downwards into a dry cement-sand mix. Both methods make paths which are rather hard on the feet but have a very pleasant visual texture. They are traditional for cottage gardens, where the owners used whatever came easily and cheaply to hand, and were revived by the Arts and Crafts movement, whose practitioners found the texture an agreeable contrast to areas of smooth stone. Many courtyards of the nineteenth century employed pitching as an alternative to granite setts, with very good effect. Because of the labour involved you will probably have to confine the effect to panels emphasizing the position of an ornament, or to the infill of a pattern largely made from another material .

Flexible Paths

The following materials are described as 'flexible' because they can be laid to any curved or sinuous shape – which would be difficult to achieve with most of the 'hard-path' materials. They all have to be retained by a firm boundary to keep them in

Path Edgings

Throughout garden history the most widely used path material has been gravel, and the necessity of retaining the path to preserve its line has been dealt with in a number of ways over the centuries.

In medieval times, garden beds were frequently raised above the level of the path and railed with trelliswork or wooden palings painted white or green. Sixteenth- and early seventeenth-century path edgings included a variety of materials, such as embattled lead, sheeps' shanks and pebbles

In the formal garden of the seventeenth century, paths were edged with Dwarf Box (*Buxus sempervirens* 'Suffruticosa'). Wooden boards were used for the ribbon walk and serpentine path of the early eighteenth-century landscape garden; later, formal stone edging was used for the flower gardens near the house.

In the proliferating suburban villas of the nineteenth-century a mass-produced path-

edging material was required, and this demand was met by tiles of various designs, notably the rope-pattern, diamond and curved top, many of which remain today. With the onset of a more informal style of gardening in the early years of the twentieth century, gravel was superseded by brick or paving paths which did not need an edging material. Grass paths were sometimes edges with stone borders to facilitate mowing.

Because of the wide variety of path edgings used throughout the centuries, it is not difficult to find authentic or good quality reproductions for your period garden today.

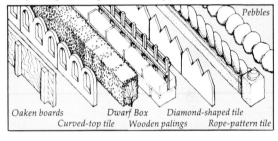

Oaken boards   *Dwarf Box*   *Diamond-shaped tile*
Curved-top tile   *Wooden palings*   *Rope-pattern tile*
Pebbles

place and prevent the edge of the path breaking away.

Originally the boundary would have been of wooden boards, held in place by pegs and replaced whenever the wood rotted. Today, with tanalized timber and many rot-proofing materials available, the problem should not be so great. However, for a permanent solution it would be better to use bricks or natural stone set on edge and held in place with cement. Small pieces of broken stone flags, set on edge with their tops kept level, or small rocks would also be suitable. The more precise edging of brick or stone flag would be used in the early pleasance and formal gardens, the romantic gardens being more likely to use rocks planted with low-growing alpines in the crevices where the path adjoins a bed.

GRAVEL

Various kinds of gravel have been used for garden paths at all periods and are suitable

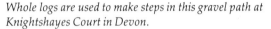

Whole logs are used to make steps in this gravel path at Knightshayes Court in Devon.

in any garden scheme. Loose gravel – shingle – is uncomfortable to walk on, and it is better to use what is called a binding gravel, or hoggin, which contains an element of clay. This is laid over a base of coarse gravel or stone and must be thoroughly rolled and watered to make a firm path. Because this results in a very sticky surface, a much finer crushed or pea gravel is rolled into the wet surface to produce a clean, dry path. Maintenance is easy with long-acting weedkillers, but care must be taken that these do not creep from the edge of the path into the adjoining lawn or beds.

STONE CHIPPINGS

Chippings of stone, marble and crushed brick have been used either for paths or, much more often, to make the background to the Box (*Buxus*) scrollwork of elaborate parterres. If used for paths the problem is to keep the material in place as, unlike the gravel, usually there is nothing but the path edging to hold it. However, hoggin can be used as the base and the chippings rolled into the surface; a light spray of tar and some more chippings ensure a firmer hold. Stone or crushed brick might have been used both for the pleasance and small-scale formal gardens in areas lacking access to supplies of gravel, but marble chips, apart from acting as the background to a parterre, only belong in an Art Deco setting.

SAND

Most of the pleasance types of garden and some of the earlier formal layouts frequently had paths of sand, but these are such a maintenance problem, since they have to be raked as well as kept weed free, that it does not seem worth reviving the idea. A very fine gravel, rolled into hoggin, will give a similar effect.

ASHES

Many of the service and other less important paths in the nineteenth-century garden were made of ashes, since these were available in vast quantities both from the house and from the boilers of the numerous greenhouses. These sources of supply no longer exist and, in any case, the paths were ugly and utilitarian. Again gravel would be nicer and equally suitable.

Soft Paths

GRASS

Grass paths have been used throughout history. They are cheap to lay and make a very attractive setting to any planting which may flank them. The disadvantages are that too much traffic turns them into mud; that they are damp to walk on in all but really dry weather; and that they need constant maintenance.

On heavy soils it is best to lay a land

This delightful grass path with double flower border at Cranbourne Manor is shown at its best in Spring.

drain through the centre of the path, falling to a suitable soakaway or outlet which rests on a layer of coarse-washed gravel. Above the drain you should spread about 15 cm (6 inches) of good soil on which the grass will grow. This will help to keep the grass dry, but it will make it inclined to brown easily during a hot summer. Bricks set on edge in concrete, their tops being about 2.5 cm (1 inch) below the finished surface of the grass, will make a neat finish and help to keep the edges in place. In the nine-teenth-century garden, grass walks passing between flower borders were generally flanked by bands of stone, similarly set below the level of the grass, so that the border plants could fall forward without getting in the way of the mowing machine.

CREEPING PLANTS

In the pleasance gardens and in the early formal garden, paths were also made of creeping plants, particularly Thyme (*Thymus drucei*), Chamomile (*Anthemis nobilis*) or Creeping Mint (*Mentha requienii*); the first two need well-drained, the latter a damp, soil. Small-rooted fragments of these plants are set into carefully prepared and weed-free soil at regular intervals, usually 15 cm (6 inches) apart, and are allowed to grow together. Such paths are pleasant to walk on, as the crushed plants give off an agreeable scent, and in theory might be supposed to be low maintenance since they require no mowing. Unfortunately, in practice, they are very labour intensive, as however careful you are, small creeping weeds which are difficult to remove get in among the plants: using chemical weedkillers is im-possible and even the smallest fork tends to bring up quantities of the path plant while leaving the weed behind. If you want to include paths of creeping plants in your garden, do so only in small areas.

Basic Path Construction

Whatever surface finish is chosen, a path always needs good foundations and proper drainage. The extent of the path should be excavated to a depth of 23 cm (9 inches), and the soil below must be consolidated. Then lay and consolidate a 15-cm (6-inch) layer of broken rubble or stone or coarse shingle 'blinded' with sand; this is spread over and worked in so that it fills all the cracks between the coarser material, and the whole is again thoroughly consolidated by being rolled, vibrated over or rammed with a heavy rammer.

The treatment above this level will de-pend on the surface finish. Stone flags are set on a bed of sand, as described, while bricks, tiles and pre-cast slabs can be laid directly on to a concrete raft, which can be given extra strength by some reinforcing rods. Where such a raft of a minimum depth of 7.5 cm (3 inches) is used, the layer of hardcore can be less. Binding gravel goes on in a 7.5-cm (3-inch) layer, since the topcoat of fine crushed gravel takes little space.

Drainage

Drainage is important and can be achieved either by giving the path a camber – that is, making it higher in the middle, so that in section the upper surface is slightly curved – or by giving it a slight fall either from end to end or side to side. You can thus direct the rain water where you want it. Cam-bered paths – generally used for the flexible or small-scale hard-surface finishes – either allow the water into adjoining planted areas through narrow gaps left in the edging, or have a land drain running down the sides of the path below ground, con-nected to catch pits with small gratings set in the edge of the path. If you have a gravel path on a steep slope, it may be necessary to have an open gulley at the sides of the path made of cobbles, pitching or some other hard material.

For hard paths, angled to a fall, the water will probably have to be directed to a rather larger catch pit with a grating, from which it must be piped away to a nearby outfall or soakaway. More precise instructions for path making can be found in books on garden construction.

Steps

Although capable of infinite variation, there are only two basic designs of step. One is made in two pieces: the riser or upright section and the tread, which overhangs it. The other is the block step in which each step is, in effect, a single block of material set one behind the other.

There is a basic formula for the proportions of steps: twice the rise, plus the depth of the tread must equal 66 cm (26 inches); for example, if you want steps with a rise of 15 cm (6 inches) – a comfortable maximum for outdoor use – then the tread will be 36 cm (14 inches) deep. If you stick to this formula within a minimum rise of 10 cm (4 inches) and a maximum of 15 cm (6 inches)

your steps will always have a good proportion. The shallower the rise the broader the flight of steps should be. If for some reason you are obliged to have really steep steps they should also be narrow, like a step ladder.

The early pleasance gardens appear always to have block steps of brick, stone or, in very simple examples, gravel held in place by wooden boards and pegs. The technique of making steps from flexible materials reappeared in this century in wild gardens, with risers made of railway sleepers or sections of split logs (much better than the earlier boards). Even grass steps, similarly made, are not unknown, but are impractical and maintenance problems rule them out.

Elaborate formal gardens of all periods had stone steps with separate treads, the oversail of which was often beautifully carved to emphasize the band of shadow below. But simpler examples and even some very grand nineteenth-century steps used blocks of stone. Baroque gardens of the late seventeenth and early eighteenth centuries made a great feature of garden stairways, the flights dividing and joining

Calculating step dimensions

When planning your steps, use the following basic formula to ensure that they will be comfortable to climb. First, choose the height of rise you require (15 cm (6 inches) is the maximum for comfortable outdoor use) and then apply this rule to find the correct depth for the tread:

Twice the height of the rise, plus the depth of the tread, must equal 66 cm (26 inches).

Examples of proportions

For example: (Rise × 2) + depth of tread = 66
In this case it has been decided that the height of the rise will be 15 cm (6 inches)

$$(15 \times 2) + \text{tread} = 66$$
$$30 + \text{tread} = 66$$
$$66-30 = 36$$

Therefore the depth of tread for a rise of 15 cm (6 inches) should be 36 cm (14 inches).

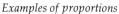

| 11 cm (4½ ins) | 44 cm (17 ins) | | 12.5 cm (5 ins) | 41 cm (16 ins) | | 14 cm (5½ ins) | 38 cm (15 ins) | | 16.5 cm (6½ ins) | 33 cm (13 ins) |

The risers of these steps are made of railway sleepers, which are kept in place by sturdy wooden pegs.

The graduated sizes of these block steps adds dignity and splendour to the design.

An elegant horseshoe-shaped flight of steps creates a period mood and is not especially difficult to construct.

again at landings furnished with fountains and statuary, while the steps themselves were frequently curved and sinuous. Such theatrical extravagance now is unlikely, but modest horseshoe-shaped flights curving around a wall fountain and perhaps fanning out at the bottom would be quite possible.

Sometimes these stairways were bounded by railings of wrought iron. At other times they were edged by stone balustrades. Fortunately these are now copied by firms who produce good-quality reproduction garden ornaments, although they are usually confined to straight flights. For a curved stairway you will probably have to have the base and handrail cast specially to fit your shape, which will prove to be expensive.

In the Arts and Crafts garden, where steps gained a new importance, the decoration was of another kind. While treads were of stone slabs – more rustic than the highly finished architecture of the formal garden – the risers were generally of brick

Shallow steps break up this paved area to make it interesting and attractive.

These steep stone steps, shrouded by roses, create a feeling of mystery in the gardens of Milton Lodge.

or layers of thin roofing tile, which added to the horizontal effect. Often the shapes of the stairways were rather eccentric; one favourite design was based on a circle which formed a landing at the middle level, the steps above getting narrower as they descended to it and those below fanning out as they fell away; or a group of circles might be combined.

Stairways of this period, usually bold and broad in conception, frequently had no balustrades at all, since the steps fanned out on all sides and did not need them. In simpler examples the stairs were recessed into retaining walls, which avoided the problem, or they were built around plant boxes. Similar bold stairways, but straight instead of curved and made from *in situ* concrete block steps set between rectangular concrete plant boxes, were very much a feature of the Art Deco gardens in the 1920s.

10
GARDEN
ORNAMENT

any of the early forms of ornamental features for the European garden had utilitarian origins. Well-, spring- and conduit-heads, dovecotes and sundials all had important functions for the household, which, as the medieval garden developed, became incorporated as ornamental centre-pieces in the layout. These objects have continued to be made for gardens long after their utilitarian functions have ceased.

Conduit-heads

The most common ornament in the medieval garden was the well-, spring- or conduit-head, sited as a centre-piece in a formal layout. It was similar to the conduit-heads or fountains in town squares or market places – water ran through spouts from a central feature and fell into a basin at or near ground level.

Heraldic Beasts

The earliest ornaments specially sculptured for the European garden were medieval or Renaissance heraldic animals; these were particularly favoured in the royal palace gardens of sixteenth-century England. In these gardens, the royal arms, made of wood or stone and usually painted in heraldic colours, were borne by heraldic beasts set on posts or pedestals.

Sundials

By the sixteenth century, the fixed sundial had also become a free-standing sculptured ornament for the garden. It was important for time-keeping and as a regulator for mechanical clocks and watches, and indeed its usefulness lasted until the railway age of the nineteenth century. Henry VIII, in his garden at Hampton Court, had no less than sixteen sundials. One of the earliest surviving free-standing examples, dating from the late sixteenth century, is in the stone quadrangle at Corpus Christi College, Oxford. It has numerous vertical dials facing in many directions; its architectural arrangement of classical base and column supporting a multi-faced dial-head, topped with a heraldic animal taken from the owner's arms, became a much-favoured design throughout the seventeenth and early eighteenth centuries. It was a design often featured in Scottish gardens, where a number of examples still exist.

From the eighteenth century onwards, the majority of garden sundials had horizontal dials on lower stone supports in the form of balusters, short columns or figures. Sometimes the support would be of marble and elegantly carved, while the balusters were carved in the architectural style of the time.

Dials for horizontal sundials were made from copper, bronze and brass, and were finely engraved. The well-proportioned dial was designed for effect, as it is with the face of a quality clock. The gnomon or style, the pointer set up to cast a shadow on the dial – it must point to the North Pole at an angle equal to the latitude of the site (or to the South Pole, in the Southern Hemisphere) – was made of the same material as the remainder of the dial.

If accurately constructed and set up, sundials show Apparent Solar Time, which differs from Mean Solar Time by an amount called the Equation of Time. This difference is due to the Earth's orbit round the sun; in other words, an ellipse. The Equation of Time reaches its maximum difference – minus some fourteen minutes in February, and plus over sixteen minutes in early November – with a zero value for only four days of the year. The exact tables for the Equation of Time for each year can be found in various almanacs, and, of course, summer time must also be taken into account when reading a sundial.

The dial of many garden sundials includes an appropriate motto, typically reflecting on life and the passing of time; for example, *One fleeth as a shadow*.

Old garden sundials can still be pur-

Centrally placed medieval well-head in cloistered courtyards at Iford Manor, Wiltshire.

Multi-faced sundial with heraldic beast finial at Barrington Court, Somerset.

chased from dealers. Reproduction and contemporary designs are also manufactured today, usually in reconstituted stone. As these designs are in a period style, particularly the baluster, it is essential to choose one in keeping with the garden and the surrounding architecture. Alternatively, a dial can be purchased from a specialised manufacturer to suit the latitude of your garden, to be mounted on a specially made support. Many stone quarries will cut stone to a design, provided they are given a scaled drawing to show your precise requirements. Most sundials are placed on a low plinth in matching stone paving.

Lead Figures
The Renaissance gardens of Italy and France were ornamented with statues and urns, carved in marble or stone by some of

the leading sculptors of the day. By the end of the seventeenth century, as it became increasingly common to surround more modest houses with pleasure gardens, sculptors could not keep up with the demand for garden statuary: it was met by the casting of figures, vases and urns in lead. Although mass-produced, the original moulds were made by eminent artists of the time, many of Flemish origin (who settled in London from the end of the seventeenth century). Leading sculptors in lead at this time were John Van Nost and later his nephew of the same name, Peter Scheemakers, Sir Henry Cheere and his younger brother. Most of their products were similar: an individual style was rare. Popular figures were shepherds, shepherdesses, gardeners, harlequins, columbines, sailors, Father Time, chubby cherubs, representations of the four seasons, and even

Pedestal-type sundial forming the centrepiece of a garden at Illmington Manor, Warwickshire.

Early eighteenth-century lead figure of a shepherd at Charlecote Park, Warwickshire.

149

'The Gamekeeper' by Cheere in painted lead, one of a number of stock patterns from the early eighteenth century.

Roman soldiers carrying firearms.

Sometimes the figures were painted in realistic clothing and hair colours. Now they are usually left unpainted to show off the patination of weathered lead or, alternatively, they are whitened to pick out any fine detail and as a contrast to a dark background of evergreen foliage: recently this has been done for the famous lead figures at Powis Castle most successfully.

Lead figures and vases from the seventeenth and eighteenth centuries are rare, but lead figures, often smaller, were made from the nineteenth century, and these are more readily available. Sometimes the leadwork is in need of repair; this should be carried out by experienced craftsmen.

Charming lead figure of Spring, probably nineteenth century, but with a timeless quality.

Lead Cisterns

Lead cisterns date from the seventeenth and eighteenth centuries. Made chiefly to collect rain water from town house roofs, they were, therefore, quite large and were usually rectangular or semi-circular for placing against a wall, although circular ones were also manufactured. All were decorated in relief work, frequently with the date of manufacture prominently displayed. These cisterns are very attractive, and the leadwork will usually have acquired a rich patina. Many gardens made during the nineteenth century or the early 1900s have one or several fine old lead cisterns. In America, very accurate copies have been reproduced, usually in lead, on a smaller scale.

If you can acquire one, the lead cistern would be very appropriate against a wall of a courtyard. Rarer circular examples make a good centre-piece for a courtyard or formal garden. They should be placed on a paved plinth, so the decoration can be more readily seen and enjoyed.

Vases and Urns

Garden urns (usually lidded) and vases (no lid) have never been out of fashion in European gardens: they have simply been arranged in different ways to complement either formal or informal layouts. In formal gardens, they were used liberally; two or more could be seen in any one view. Because of their associated feeling of melancholy they were also used singly in the landscape garden, where the beautifully proportioned handmade objects acted as a focal point in a minor scene. (Something on the scale of a garden building would have been used for a larger composition.)

Urns and vases have been inspired by classical art, and many copies on various scales have been made from Roman de-

Eighteenth-century cisterns were usually made for town courtyards, but became popular as garden ornaments.

signs; the most notable of these is the Warwick Vase, found in 1770 in the bed of a lake at Hadrian's Villa, near Tivoli. Classical vases were chiefly made from marble or stone. The Renaissance continued this tradition, and some superb vases in marble were made for the gardens of the Palace of Versailles. Vases and urns were also cast in metal, notably bronze and lead; the latter metal was much cheaper and therefore more common in late seventeenth- and eighteenth-century gardens, while stone was also much favoured during this period.

One of the most successful cheaper products in Britain was Coade ware, the precise formula of which is not known now. But it was very successful, being

A Renaissance Roof Garden

The Renaissance garden relied heavily on architectural ornament and container planting for its impact, which makes it a good style to adapt for an urban roof garden – ideal for the busy town dweller who wants to enjoy a 'garden' with minimum maintenance. (Before you begin, check with a surveyor as to whether your flat roof is suitable for this purpose).

The most important element of the Renaissance garden was stone balustrading, now available from manufacturers of reconstituted stone products in seventeenth-century designs. Although this may initially be more expensive than the basic railings required to meet safety standards, the result will be one of classical and enduring beauty rather than mere utility. If you have the opportunity to make two levels by introducing a flight of steps it will add considerably to the Renaissance ambience.

Decorate the balustrading at intervals with stone vases planted with ivy to soften the architectural effect. As a concession to the twentieth century these could be filled with trailing ivy-leaved geraniums to add colour throughout the summer months. Pot-grown evergreens placed at regular intervals will give the garden its year-round interest – citrus trees grown in formal square tubs were a favourite with seventeenth-century gardeners, as were mop-headed Bay trees or cone-shaped Box topiary.

Statuary was a prominent feature of the Renaissance garden, so animate the roofscape with a figure from classical mythology – Neptune, Cupid or a graceful nymph. Antique statuary is exorbitantly expensive but some beautiful reproductions, made of reconstituted marble, are imported from Italy. Siting is dependent on the individual situation, but use your imagination – even a capped chimney can make an unusual plinth.

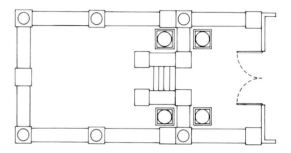

A flat roof could supply the ideal setting for a roof garden in the Renaissance style, which relied on architectural ornament and container planting for its impact.

more resistant to weathering than many quarried stones, with designs of a high standard. (Besides vases and monuments, Coade stone was used for the manufacture of sphinxes and a range of architectural mouldings.)

From the end of the eighteenth century, various forms of artificial stone were used for garden vases and urns. In addition, vases were made in well-fired ceramic wares. But by the 1850s, cast iron had become the most common material for mass-producing garden vases. These vases were normally manufactured with a cast iron base, which had matching decorative motifs.

During the nineteenth century, flower vases for the garden were also made from wrought iron; straps and hoops were formed into an openwork vase. For planting, the vase would first be lined with moss, as in a wirework hanging basket.

Vases rather than urns remain a popular ornament today. They are mostly cast in artificial stone, with varying degrees of success. As always, the poor quality castings lack crispness in the representation of carved decorations – some look too much like common concrete – and certainly a casting in artificial stone does not have the attractive grain of natural stone. When choosing one of these reproductions, look

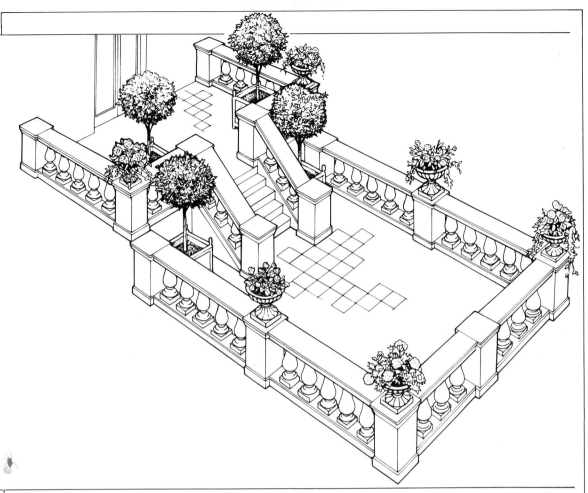

for quality of manufacture and pick an example that is in style with the period of the garden or balustrading or, if placed near the house, the architecture of the building.

Fine old carved stone examples, as well as finely modelled terracotta vases and examples cast in lead, are available from specialists, but they are expensive. Lower down the price range are the cast iron examples which, because of the material, will have a nineteenth-century feel about them and so are suited to gardens and situations of this era.

A sumptuously carved Italian stone vase at Tyninghame, East Lothian.

Nineteenth-century Italian Garden Ornaments

During the second half of the eighteenth century in Britain, the setting desired by country house owners was a pastoral one, which the landscape park so successfully provided. By the end of the century, the English park had become the fashionable style of gardening in large areas of northern Europe and the United States of America.

However, this was also the time when new flowering plants were introduced from various parts of the world, notably bedding plants such as pelargoniums from South Africa. By the end of the nineteenth century garden owners wished to grow the fascinating new range of exotics. The style of layout first adapted for this new gardening was the Italian formal garden: its level terraces supporting flower beds in full light were ideal for these flowers.

But the Italian style of gardening required stone ornaments, balustrading and stairways. As a result of this new fashion, many garden ornaments, inspired by classical art, were manufactured and imported from Italy. Besides stone statuary and vases, there were some uniquely Italian ornaments exported throughout this period and into the early years of the twentieth century. The most characteristic Italian export was the stone and wrought iron well-head. The standard design consisted of a stone base, elegantly shaped, sometimes undercut and richly carved. Set into the base was a decorated wrought iron crane and windlass. These well-heads make an attractive centre-piece to a small Victorian or Edwardian formal garden or paved courtyard situated close to the house, and they are sometimes available from suppliers of quality garden ornaments.

This stone urn with companion owl makes an evocative ornament in La Pietra, Italy.

Sculptural group suitable for an informal part of a Victorian garden.

Bird Baths

Water provision for birds was a fashion which developed in early twentieth-century suburban gardens, where bird-lovers wished to attract and see wild birds. Birds need water not only for drinking, but also for bathing; so it must be shallow water – hence the stone or lead bird bath, frequently supported on a pedestal to provide greater security from a pouncing cat. Lead bird baths of this period had decorated sides and often a bird cast in lead attached to the rim. For small pre-Second World War gardens within view of the house, these bird baths can make an attractive period feature.

Sculpture

While there is no clear distinction between statuary and sculpture, the latter term, as far as garden ornament is concerned, is associated with sculptured figures specially made for gardens in the contemporary style of the time. The demand for modern sculpture, as against vernacular art, started in the Art Nouveau garden and continued up to the 1960s. This period includes work from some of the leading sculptors of the day, as for example Henry Moore's *Reclining Figure* in the gardens at Dartington Hall. This kind of sculpture is very much of the age in which it was made, and will only satisfactorily fit into a garden of the same period.

Japanese Garden Ornaments

An important part of the Japanese garden is the use of carefully selected rocks and ornaments. During the twelfth century, influenced by Zen Buddhism, the Japanese garden became a dry landscape, composed largely of rocks, graded stones and raked sand.

The Zen masters aimed to infuse natural

A modern lead figure of a crane, suitable for many types of period garden.

objects with spiritual values, which would release the mind from worldly thoughts and promote a sense of inner peace. In an enclosed, simple and serene dry garden, the rocks, carefully chosen for shape, colour and growth of mosses and lichens, symbolized mountains, islands or other aspects of nature; the sand, which might represent the sea or streams, was raked into symbolic patterns, differing according to the time of the year. Later Japanese gardens became less austere, were larger and supported more plants, with still, reflective water, garden buildings, ornaments and facilities for the tea ceremony.

The most frequently used ornamental item was the stone lantern, which originated as a votive lantern offered to Shinto or

Japanese garden showing a well-sited lantern: Newstead Abbey, Nottinghamshire.

Terracotta vase in basket-weave pattern, which was a popular style during the Victorian period.

Buddhist deities. Later low-level illumination was provided to parts of the garden by the burning of candles or seed oil inside the lantern. In more recent times a large range of lantern designs has been available for use as ornaments carefully sited within a garden scene.

The traditional lantern design consists of a low plinth, a pedestal varying in height from a few centimetres to a metre (an inch to 3 feet) to support the lantern housing, a curved shaped roof and a finial. The best examples in the West were imported from Japan at about the turn of the century and are usually in granite. Inferior cast copies have also been made, together with some acceptable carved reproductions.

Terracotta Pots

Decorative terracotta pots were first used in large numbers in the Renaissance gardens in Italy. Since that time they have never been totally out of fashion, and have continued to be made by a succession of potters. Their period feel or association with a particular style of garden depends very much on their decoration. Basket-weave patterns are associated with early nineteenth-century flower gardens, lion-heads and swags go with formal classical gardens of any date, and Victorian motifs of flowers and foliage, such as ivy, will look best in gardens of that period.

A popular ornament for small gardens at the turn of the century was the undecorated oil or Ali Baba-type jar, which relied on its good pottery outline for visual appeal.

The one golden rule to follow in buying terracotta pots is to ensure that they are well fired and therefore able to resist any local frost damage. Many examples are machine-made and can lack crispness in the modelling. However there are a small number of potters today still throwing and decorating traditional garden pots of fine quality which compare favourably with the machine-made imports.

11
GARDEN FURNITURE

In making a period garden, the aim will normally be to recreate the spirit of a particular period. But the garden should not be a museum and, for instance, the very temporary nature of modern garden furniture designed for relaxation, providing it is portable, will not greatly interfere with the spirit of the period garden. However, for permanent furniture, the siting, style and materials will be as important to the mood as they are to a period room.

Turf Seats

The earliest piece of furniture in Europe designed specifically for the garden was the turf seat. Medieval gardens were enclosed areas, sometimes resembling outdoor rooms; the layout was formal with raised geometrically shaped beds bounded by a pattern of gravel paths. A bed would sometimes run the length of an enclosing wall, with the soil retained by a wattle of interwoven osiers, or by masonry. Such a bed would be turfed with grass out of which flowers would grow. At intervals along the raised bed, sections of low-grown flowers would mark off a turf seat. As late as 1618, William Lawson recommended, in his *New Orchard and Garden*, that 'camamile, penny-royal, daisies and violets are seemly and comfortable' for seats. The turf seat is occasionally shown in contemporary pictures as a single raised bed, which was sometimes developed to form a covered bower, made from timber latticework supporting climbing or trained plants. Illustrations of turf seats in medieval gardens can be found in manuscripts, such as the Flemish *Romaunt de la Rose*. Chaucer gave the following description of one of these seats:

> That benched was, and all with turves new
> Freshly turved, whereof the green gras
> So small, so thick, so short, so fresh of hew,
> That most like to grene wool, wot I, it was.

While it is reasonably easy to construct a turf seat, its usefulness is restricted to the very driest weeks of the year. Today, its value would only be in its novelty and in its contribution to a 'period' mood.

Renaissance Stone Garden Seats

The superb Italian Renaissance gardens of the sixteenth century fully utilized the skills of stonemasons, who constructed many garden features – steps, walls and balustrades, for example. Because of the climate, turf had no place in these gardens, and seats fashioned from stone fitted into the ground plans with their classically proportioned and moulded stonework. Sometimes a relatively simple stone or marble bench was set in a garden recess, or perhaps it was of a more elaborate design with carved ends to the seat supports and the back.

The stone or marble seat was often curved to reflect the overall shape of the formal plan or to act as a feature at the end of a vista. In the mid-nineteenth century

Recreated turf seat in the herb garden at Sissinghurst, Kent. They make interesting, if impractical, features.

One of a rather grand pair of eighteenth-century marble garden seats, now hard to find.

the formal garden, with a strong Italian flavour, had a great revival in Europe and parts of North America, and many stone and some marble neo-classical seats manufactured in Italy were exported to the rest of Europe. They were also made in Britain, where Bath stone was a favourite material. These seats are suitable not only for Italian-style gardens, but also for terraces and balustraded areas adjoining houses of classical design.

Since the end of the Second World War, classical benches and seats have been cast in reconstituted stone. The edge of the seat will normally have some decorative moulding and the plinth-type supports may be carved as a seated lion. Because of the very high cost of cutting and fashioning anything in stone, it may be necessary to resort to these reconstructions when recreating a formal garden. However, only the best quality manufacturers should be considered, and the seat itself should be viewed rather than relying on photographs in the catalogue. Generally, cast stone lacks the crispness of carved examples and therefore a simple design will be the most convincing.

Chinese Garden Seats

At least as early as the beginning of the sixteenth century the Chinese evolved a garden seat; it was made in porcelain and beautifully decorated. The shape was based on that of a drum and had borders of studs – replicas of the pins securing the drum skin – around the top and bottom. Frequently the side was pierced and lions' heads or rings were often included for lifting the seat. There is no evidence that these were exported to Europe until the nineteenth century and any examples made before this date will be extremely rare and likely to be displayed indoors. The

A Chinese porcelain garden seat, many of which were imported into Europe in the 1800s for use in conservatories.

export examples can still be found, however, and add to the atmosphere of a conservatory; on no account should they be left unprotected from frost.

These Chinese seat designs were also produced in stone with more rotund matching drum tables. Several seats placed around such a table have a marvellous sculptural quality.

Timber Seats of the Eighteenth and Early Nineteenth Centuries

House furniture in the eighteenth and early nineteenth centuries in Europe and North America reached, and sustained, a very high quality. The designs went through a series of well recognized styles, which were closely followed by the designers of timber garden furniture. Although little of this has survived to the present day – the exceptions are the furniture protected in garden buildings, porticos and covered alcoves – it is well recorded in pattern-books of the day. Occasionally the furniture was designed by leading architects from the metropolitan areas, but mostly it was made by local artisans and estate carpenters, from pattern-books produced by leading furniture designers.

Patterns for seats and chairs meant for furnishing garden buildings in the classical, Chinese or Gothic styles are often included. Classical garden buildings with matching furniture were popular throughout the period, but there was a certain mid-eighteenth-century vogue for Chinese pagodas, kiosks and other garden structures – a style very much the European idea of Chinese garden architecture and decoration, now generally referred to as chinoiserie. The furniture was likely to be built in a traditional European framework but with Chinese decoration and perhaps colouring. Usually the seats or chairs had back rails arranged in a characteristically angled Chinese style – this was a feature of the furniture manufactured by Thomas Chippendale – and sometimes the timber was shaped to simulate bamboo. The furniture was coloured to match the Chinese buildings: red or turquoise with perhaps some gilding was particularly popular. The 'Chinese Chippendale' pattern for the back railing has remained a favourite seat design for the garden. There is a particularly strong tradition for this type of garden seat in period or recreated period gardens in Virginia, USA, notably in the charming gardens behind the Colonnades at the University of Virginia, Charlottesville, and at Colonial Williamsburg.

A taste for the Gothic in architecture, interior decoration and garden buildings developed alongside that for chinoiserie. Gothick designers produced a wide range of mood furniture – from bizarre rustic to pointed backs filled in with traditional

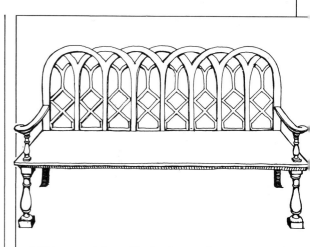

A Chinese seat, from Charles Over's 'Ornamental Architecture in the Gothic Chinese and Modern Taste', 1758.

decoration of quatrefoils and branching tracery patterns.

These seats are rare and will seldom come on the market. However, they can be reproduced from the engravings in pattern-books, such as Charles Over's *Ornamental Architecture in the Gothic, Chinese and Modern Taste* (1758); Robert Manwaring's *The Cabinet and Chair-Maker's Real Friend and Companion* (1765); William and John Halfpenny's *New Designs for Chinese Temples* (1750), and William Chambers's *Designs of Chinese Buildings, Furniture, Dresses, Machines and Utensils* (1757).

These designs can be modified and simplified to suit individual taste or the available budget. Usually, the seats were made of oak or a similar hardwood. If oak is used it can be left to weather to an attractive silvery grey colour. Placed within a garden building, portico or loggia, the seats were often painted in a colour to blend with the building's interior. Other woods used were yew, apple and pear, especially for rustic seats which were fashioned to appear as if made from bran-

Rustic chairs, from Robert Manwaring's 'The Cabinet and Chairmaker's Real Friend and Companion', 1765.

This timber seat at Colonial Williamsburg is in the 'Chinese Chippendale' style.

ches still supporting leaves and blossom; it was recommended that these seats be painted 'to appear like Nature'.

In the early years of the nineteenth century, new designs for furniture appeared at more frequent intervals. Much of the inspiration came from newly discovered designs from Ancient Greece and Egypt, and from the military and naval campaigns of the Napoleonic Wars, which gave rise to sabre-shaped legs and nautical details in rope-patterned rails. Garden furniture design in timber was influenced by these fashions, and there are examples, for instance, of sabre-legged seats.

Fine seats built from these period patterns should be placed on paving or even a platform, to ensure a dry situation. Alternatively, they can be given more protection in a garden building, portico or loggia. Any algae growth should be cleaned away regularly and, if painted, they must be repainted at least every other year. In the past the unpainted wood would have been given annual applications of linseed oil; boiled if it was teak, and unboiled for oak.

Wrought Iron Seats

During the eighteenth and nineteenth centuries, the local blacksmith produced and kept in repair an enormous range of utilitarian objects, as well as some decorative work, including garden seats. Wrought iron was especially suited for this purpose, having greater resistance to weathering than timber. The wrought iron seat is unique to the garden, and has an elegance and lightness. Traditionally, the seat is made entirely of the same material, with curves contrasting with straight pieces. In the better quality examples the flat ironwork was given a reeded finish, which added to the elegance of line, and perhaps lion-paw feet. The most usual designs were for single chairs, with or without arms, and bench seats and circular seats with backs, the latter for fitting around the bole of a tree.

Modern attempts at reproducing these seats are successful when restrained designs are adopted, but usually mild steel is used instead of wrought iron: the steel must be well galvanized and properly painted against rusting. When the new material is bent into curls to imitate the wrought curl, it is generally unconvincing: it is best to avoid this favourite detail of modern imitators in any case, as it was not often used in seat designs.

Wrought ironwork in the garden was always painted to protect it from rusting. To make the most of the seat's elegant outline, it should be painted matt white and be placed against a dark background, such as a yew hedge. Other traditional colours, suitable for lighter backgrounds, are black, ordnance blue (a dark blue which is almost black), turquoise blue and chocolate – all with a matt finish.

In the nineteenth century, several ingeniously designed single chairs were manufactured, with more comfortable seats that had some 'give' to them, or were even sprung. These surprisingly easy seats were made out of flat chains, or interwoven metal straps and a chainmail-like netting filled the frame of both the seat and the

The interlacing metal straps on the seat of this wrought iron garden chair give a comfortable 'sprung' effect.

A modern, decorative iron tree seat in a garden in Alkerton, Oxfordshire, showing good use of the material.

This wrought iron seat has a folding foot rest and wheels which enable it to be moved about the garden.

back support. The ultimate design had a round, convex seat made up of flexible straps of metal curved and sprung where they joined the seat frame, and meeting at a circular centre-piece. The back also had sprung metal bands joined at the back of the seat frame and at a cross member near the top of the balloon-shaped back. They were made with or without curved wrought iron arms, and were sometimes joined up to make two- or three-seaters. Many of these attractive balloon-back garden chairs were manufactured in France and Britain; those that have survived are rather prized, and are most likely now to be given the protection of the conservatory or loggia.

William Robinson, the 'father of the English flower garden', was much taken with these delightful garden chairs, and included them in his book *The Parks, Promenades and Gardens of Paris* (1869), recording that they were 'seen in quantities in all public places in Paris'. Robinson

also mentions a garden chair of similar outline which had a sprung seat made from thin interwoven metal straps.

A good range of metal chairs and bench seats, hardwearing and weatherproof, are manufactured in the USA; some of these are very suitable for a period mood in a garden. A number of designs closely resemble the chairs of the eighteenth and nineteenth centuries, while many have very comfortable seats made from an interwoven mesh of wirework or chainwork.

Covered Seats

As the enjoyment of flower gardens grew in the nineteenth century, ingenious shades were designed for garden seats placed in sunny positions. The decorative tent canopies erected over a seat for the summer months were not too dissimilar from the umbrella seat that was shown in some eighteenth century pattern-books; Charles Over's *Ornamental Architecture*, for instance. Then, the canopy was probably

An elegant wrought iron seat made in the traditional style with curves contrasting with straight lines.

These Edwardian wrought iron and chain mesh garden chairs can be folded up for easy storage.

meant to be in copper and, in keeping with the seat beneath, was in Chinese taste. Fifty years later, period canvas was preferred and the characteristic sabre-legged furniture was in vogue. The architect John B. Papworth illustrates a very elegant covered seat in this style in his *Rural Residences* (1832). In the second half of the nineteenth century a lattice canopy and a plant box, to enable climbing plants to cover and shade the occupants in summer, were added to wirework seats, while standard cast iron seats were often equipped with an adjustable canvas canopy.

Wirework Furniture

New and cheaper methods of manufacturing in the nineteenth century produced various thicknesses of wire, which was made into a range of useful garden products, including some unique furniture. The wire was bent into attractive tracery patterns and wired together at the intersections to give some rigidity, on a supporting slim iron framework. In the 1851 Great Exhibition catalogue, an extensive range of garden chairs, seats, tables and flower stands was advertised; within a few years some ingenious pieces were on sale – the garden equivalent of the armchair-cum-library steps, for example, used for reaching the higher shelves or hanging baskets in the conservatory.

Seats were usually made for two people and had high backs of curving wirework: the seat itself would be well shaped to give a good comfortable support. Table legs were often in a centre tripod form and shaped to resemble three serpents. Flower stands to take a row of pot plants were a most popular piece of garden wirework; these have most often survived and are sometimes available from specialist dealers. For a period that, in comparison with

J. B. Papworth's design for a covered garden seat.

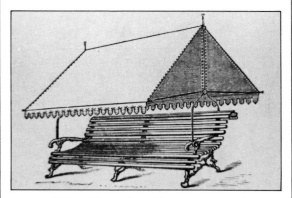

A seat of 1869 with an adjustable canvas sunshade.

A Victorian garden arbour and seat made in cast iron.

A modern octagonal rustic seat at Wroxton Abbey.

Balloon-back garden chairs and wirework flower stand.

A moveable two-seater with arbour.

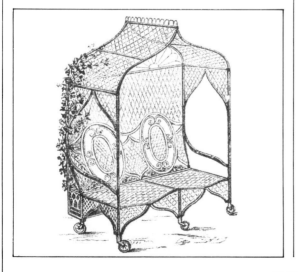

the eighteenth and early nineteenth centuries, produced such heavy and clumsy-looking furniture for the house, it is something of a surprise to discover the lightness of this wirework garden furniture.

One of the most enchanting pieces was a movable two-seater with arbour. It was mounted on six castors and had its own plant trough at the back, from which a climbing plant could be grown to cover the wirework roof of the arbour.

Rustic Furniture

Rustic chairs, seats and tables made up from sawn branches of larch or even yew wood have always been made for the garden. Landscape gardening of the eighteenth century used such furniture, as well as the hermit's hut or the root house, to evoke a variety of moods. For the hermit, real or imaginary, the rustic furniture would have an element of the grotesque about it; a central table was often hewn from a burred section of the bole of an elm. A scattering of bones and a profusion of cobwebs, all illuminated by a low, diffuse window lighting, helped to create the feeling for the sublime.

In the late nineteenth-century flower gardens, rustic furniture was much in fashion for the more natural woodland settings. Polygonal seats to surround a tree bole were popular, and decorative arrangements of branches, such as a criss-cross pattern, were usually given to the back of the seat.

Rustic furniture will last a surprising number of years if it is placed on a well-drained surface, such as gravel. It is relatively cheap to make, and will have its place in informal parts of a period garden. Always take the time to draw out an appropriate design before going ahead with the actual constructions.

Cast Iron Furniture

Cast iron is admirably suited for all-the-year-round use in the garden, for it is rust-resistant and is heavy enough not to be blown over. However, wrought iron is less brittle.

While wrought iron furniture was made by the estate or local blacksmith, cast ironwork was a product of large manufacturers. Once a pattern was made, many casts could be produced by a foundry and dispatched to any part of the country by the new railway networks: the pattern-book was replaced by the manufacturer's illustrated catalogue, sometimes a very bulky affair. An extraordinary number of items was available from major foundries – garden seats, seat-ends, tables, bootscrapers and directional signs (to the conservatory, for instance), as well as whole kiosks and arbours.

Except for the smaller two-seaters, the ironwork on garden seats was restricted to the seat-ends, with timber members making up the curved seat and back. One of the most popular seats was the fern pattern, where the back and side arm supports were cast iron fronds. It was produced from about 1850 onwards throughout the nineteenth century, and reproduced in this century for the parks and public open spaces of Stockholm. Interestingly, the manufacturer's catalogue records that this seat could be supplied painted in green, chocolate or bronzed. Today we are perhaps more likely to paint a decorative cast iron garden seat white, to show it off to its maximum effect – a trend that dates from this century rather than the last.

Another attractive and successful cast iron seat design, with quatrefoils and tracery motifs, was the Gothic pattern. Other popular Victorian design motifs, such as ivy, vines and brambles, were used, or curving serpents and overall designs imitating rustic work.

In addition to seats, cast iron was used to produce quantities of tables for hotels and public houses, conservatories, summerhouses and loggias. The most common design consisted of a circular top made from teak, or sometimes marble, supported by three shaped and decorated cast iron legs bolted together under the top and

The fern pattern in this cast iron seat was extremely popular during the second half of the nineteenth century.

Rustic-patterned cast iron seats have remained popular since their introduction in the nineteenth century.

again half way down to a pierced shelf. A wide variety of motifs was used for the decorative ironwork, from heads of river gods, goddesses, rams and lotus flowers to some notable contemporary heroes.

Cast iron tables, and to a lesser extent, garden seats with cast iron ends, are still available from specialist dealers, as are many examples of later castings of Victorian seat-ends. Recently, manufacturers have turned to aluminium castings of decorative cast iron patterns. But the thinness of many aluminium castings detracts from the period feel; they appear to be what they are – an inferior imitation. In addition, not all the original patterns for cast iron seats are attractive, unlike those for wrought iron, and not always the best designs have been chosen for recent reproduction.

Layers of old paint can be removed from old cast iron garden furniture; a de-rusting agent should be applied prior to priming and repainting. The primer should be lead-based and followed by undercoating and then at least two coats of good quality top matt.

Steamship Furniture

By the end of the nineteenth century, life at sea had become considerably more comfortable for passengers than it had been. Chairs for relaxing on deck in comfort, which could be quickly stowed away, became standard equipment on passenger ships. The steamer chair preceded the ubiquitous timber and canvas deck chair and for comfort it was a superior piece of furniture: elegant and stylish, it supported the body well, and when equipped with cushions, was admirable for long periods of relaxation; in addition, it could be folded flat for easy storage. The seat and back were usually made of beech with curved slats, or else canework was used. Some versions had a foot rest to add further length and comfort. These chairs soon became popular for use in the garden. Steamer chairs still come on the market at house sales and are well worth acquiring for their comfort and convenience.

The deck chair, a simplification of the steamer chair, is still manufactured and so will blend in to any period garden of the nineteenth or twentieth century. One other

This cast iron and timber seat was made for the Victorian railway, but can give period flavour to a garden.

A Victorian cast iron table with teak top, probably made for public houses, but suitable for the garden.

piece of garden furniture with a nautical origin is the hammock. Made of green canvas and rope, or all rope, it is usually tied up between two trees, which provide shade. Equipped with cushions, it is a luxurious piece of garden furniture.

Terracotta and Ceramic Seats

Italy manufactured and exported a great deal of garden furniture and ornament. Besides stone seats, the late nineteenth-century exports included some classically inspired terracotta seats, designed with a horseshoe-shaped drum base and a low decorated rim in place of an actual back

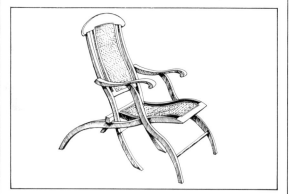

The steamer chair, popular in late Victorian gardens.

support. Attractive modelling, usually figureheads at the front two corners and a mask head in the centre of the back rim, was always of high quality. Terracotta is a reddish earthenware; the seats varied from pink to purple-red. They are best suited for classical garden buildings, and, of course, for Italian-style formal gardens.

During the nineteenth century, a few manufacturers made ceramic seats, in imitation of rustic work. The firing was of a high standard, well able to withstand frost and other weathering agents. They have a strong Victorian character and suit the informality of a wild garden.

Timber Seats, 1900-1939

The British architect Sir Edwin Lutyens, who created gardens of some formality near the house, with the flowers planted within this framework arranged in an informal manner, favoured white painted timber for such features as gates and seats. The latter frequently had a high, curved back, a decorated front rail and a shaped or patterned arrangement of rails for the back.

A peculiar movable seat was also popular at this time: it had a wheelbarrow wheel at one end and two handles at the other, enabling it to be easily moved about the garden.

A classical style garden table with robust supports.

A number of teak seats manufactured today are of excellent construction, but their design is a little pedestrian compared with the seats made earlier this century. Then, there was a recognizable 'style': the back and perhaps the front seat frame was shaped, and the back rails were decorated.

Loggia Furniture

Late nineteenth- and early twentieth-century country house owners furnished their loggias with soft, comfortable chairs for the summer months. Wickerwork armchairs were popular, including some with high balloon-shaped backs. The wickerwork and the framework of these chairs are vulnerable to woodworm, making inspection and insecticide treatment an important part of their maintenance. These chairs continue to be manufactured in large numbers and interesting designs.

A particularly handsome, foldable chaise-longue for the loggia was made from iron, with brass decoration and finials, interwoven flat steel bands for the springing, white ceramic castors, and three horsehair palliasses for a firm but comfortable support. This admirable chaise-longue occasionally turns up in house sales and is a splendid piece of loggia furniture.

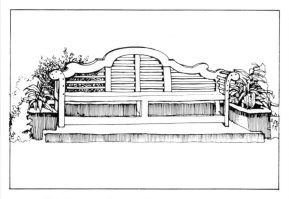

A grand timber seat designed by Sir Edwin Lutyens.

Siting of Seats

A decorative seat should act as a piece of sculpture, with a special place or niche of its own – as a focal point at the end of a vista, for instance. Mrs Loudon, in her *Ladies' Companion to the Flower Garden* (1844), stresses the importance of keeping rustic-type seats in the most naturalistic parts of the garden, and that 'seats for a lawn or highly kept pleasure garden ought to be of comparatively simple and architectural forms, and either of wood or stone'.

A formal architectural garden in the Italianate style of the nineteenth century is best furnished with stone seats or benches in a material and style to match the stonework of the balustrades, paving and steps.

For the early landscape garden, designed as a pictorial circuit route, seats were an important element of the design, and would be placed at ideal positions for viewing and admiring the landscape composition. The longer the stay intended at a particular scene, the more important the seat, graduating from a simple bench to a seat within an arbour and, most grandly, within a stone temple. At his own garden at The Leasowes, Halesowen, William Shenstone, poet, landscape theorist and practitioner, had no fewer than thirty-nine

The wheelbarrow seat was popular early in this century.

seats from which the visitor could admire, ponder and philosophize over the view. To add to the various moods that the landscape might evoke, lines of poetry, mottoes and dedications would be inscribed on the seat. Although the lesser view would only be provided with 'common benches', nevertheless the spot was marked and the spectator given a strong hint to pause and enjoy the contrived view. 'Natural bowers' were used for other seats, and for all the major views there was a seat unique to that position: a Gothic seat, for example, a seat in a Temple of Pan, an octagonal seat, a root seat and a pyramidal seat.

12
GARDEN BUILDINGS

N o other area of building has produced such original and exquisite designs as those for the garden and park: temples, pagodas and garden tombs represent some of the supreme examples in Greek, Roman, Chinese and Moghul architecture. Of the major styles, only Gothic failed to produce interesting garden buildings, although the style was more successful during its revival in the eighteenth century, when it provided an alternative to the popular classical and chinoiserie styles.

Dovecotes

A pigeon house or dovecote was one of the oldest outbuildings to a manor house. Designed for the rearing of fledgling pigeons (or squabs), they provided welcome fresh meat during the winter months. An especially heavy bird was raised, with a prolific breeding rate.

A large dovecote contained many hundreds of nesting boxes arranged as recesses in the internal walls. Access to the nesting boxes was usually from a revolving ladder in the centre of the building. For security reasons, the dovecote was commonly sited near to the house, and it was frequently incorporated into early garden layout as a centre-piece.

The earliest dovecote had a circular plan, with an anti-rat rim between the vertical walls and the dome or cone-shaped roof. Surviving Norman dovecotes have a covered opening at the apex of the dome for the birds; later this developed into a timber lantern with projecting alighting boards. From the Renaissance period, rectangular and polygonal plans were often employed. By the second half of the eighteenth century, farming methods had improved and there was little need to rear young pigeons for food. The buildings survived as interesting and perhaps nostalgic features in the garden.

Any dovecotes built after this time were purely ornamental, housing decorative kinds of doves, usually white and slender. The new ornamental dovecotes were much smaller and frequently were not separate buildings, but lofts in existing outhouses;

Gazebo at Nymans, Sussex, built in Tudor style with a dovecote at the top and a summerhouse below.

One of a pair of Elizabethan garden pavilions at Montacute House, Somerset, in Renaissance style.

sometimes they were attached to buildings or independently supported on a pedestal. The small garden dovecote constructed in timber was a particularly popular form of garden ornament at the turn of the nineteenth century. A popular design was in white-painted timber housing several nest boxes, each with its own opening and alighting board, and supported by a timber pedestal.

Banqueting Houses

These often fanciful buildings were common to important houses in the late sixteenth century and continued to be built until the eighteenth century.

The origins of the banquet go back to the medieval ceremony of the Void, the name given to the interval when the great hall or chamber was prepared for after-dinner activities. To fill this time, wine and a variety of sweet delicacies and fruit were served. By the sixteenth century, there were special rooms or turrets on the roof for this event. The end-of-the-century fashion was to have a banqueting house built in the garden where delicacies could be served not only after meals but at any time of the day. These ranged from one small room to a 'retreat' building with several storeys and containing bedrooms, kitchen and store rooms.

The banqueting houses were built in the prevailing architectural taste of the time, often reflecting, rather more fancifully, the motifs – such as pinnacles, roof line and window design – of the nearby house. Siting was given much consideration, especially the approach from the main house and the view from the banqueting house windows; it was frequently given an elevated position.

While most of the surviving examples of garden banqueting houses are in stone or brick, they can be built in timber and, of course, used as a summerhouse as well as for after-dinner drinks and delicacies.

Orangeries and Conservatories

Orange trees, with their scented blossom and fruits and evergreen foliage, are beautiful as well as productive garden plants. The desire to grow them in gardens outside their natural climatic zone led to two distinct features in Renaissance gardens. The trees were grown in large terracotta pots or timber tubs, and displayed in a special formal garden or along a terrace during the summer months; in winter, if the climate was severe, the plants were moved to some protective enclosure.

These early buildings became known as conservatories or orangeries and, during the seventeenth and eighteenth centuries, they looked more like garden buildings than glasshouses: windows were plentiful on the southern elevations, but invariably the roof was tiled. Towards the end of the eighteenth century, when it was realized that more light during the winter months was beneficial to the plants, most orangeries 'and conservatories were given glazed roofs. Heating was by means of an outside furnace; flues under the floors and in the walls conveyed the hot air through the building.

The introduction of other more light-demanding plants, such as pelargoniums, hastened the change to overall glazing.

During the nineteenth century, many

Orangery interior, Margam Park, West Glamorgan. If grown in tubs, citrus trees can be put outside in summer.

houses, large and small, contained conservatories as distinct from glasshouses; they acted as a winter garden and could be entered directly from the house. As glass became cheaper, cast iron structural members were mass-produced, and manufacturers offered complete 'kit-set' designs.

Many conservatories were very decorative. The glazed sides might have rounded bars at the top, roof ridges were sometimes given decorative iron finials, doorways were emphasized in an architectural manner, or the whole construction might have an elegant curvilinear roof span. The glazing would not normally extend to the ground, but would stop about dado level, where timber or a masonry wall provided solidity and hid hot-water pipes and the

undersides of the staging that supported the pot plants. Doors from the house to the conservatory often had a large central pane of glass surrounded by small panes of coloured glass, with some having etched patterns of conservatory flowers such as fuchsias. Mostly the conservatories were heated sufficiently to keep out frost, but no hotter. Recently, because of the cost of heating, conservatories have tended to become cold houses, but still are able to provide a climate whereby some plants can continue flowering into the winter months or start up again early in the spring.

Although the number of conservatories has diminished since the Second World War, interest has been renewed and a number of manufacturers now offer old

This solidly built conservatory is of the Victorian period, when it was fashionable to cultivate exotic plants.

designs with a nineteenth-century flavour about them. The best designs will not be cheap, but are a worthwhile investment if they are to be attached to a fine house. For important situations it will be better to have a conservatory specially designed by an experienced architect.

Temples and Pavilions

Most garden temples were directly inspired by the examples in the classical world. To the ancient Greeks and Romans, temples were the shrines for the immortal gods. 'The design of a temple depends on symmetry, the principles of which must be carefully observed by the architect,' wrote Vitruvius, the Roman architect of the first century BC. He explains these principles, as well as optical corrections and suggestions for siting, in his *Ten Books on Architecture*. From the Italian Renaissance onwards, such satisfying symmetrical structures were the perfect inspiration for garden buildings in both formal and informal settings.

The form of the temple depended on whether it was to be seen in the round (that is, from all directions) or merely from a frontal or three-quarters view. For the first position the rotunda form is used, where the columns are arranged in a circle to support a circular entablature and a domed roof. Although this is a simple concept, its successful execution is difficult to achieve: the proportions and the curve of the dome have to be in perfect harmony. The Rotunda at Stowe in Buckinghamshire, is an example of a temple perfectly proportioned for the site. When it was first built, however, the owner was not happy with the curve of the dome and it had to be altered to achieve its present success.

The designs for temples seen from one side concentrated on a columned porch or

The Temple of Fame at Studley Royal is of the rotunda form, typical of the eighteenth century.

An eighteenth-century design for a garden pavilion by Le Rouge, taken from one of his 'cahiers', circa 1770.

portico with a pediment above. Indeed, some garden temples are only porticos, providing sheltered seating for a special view as well as a focal point in the garden scene.

Stone, stucco and painted timber have all been used in the construction of garden temples. Standard kits of fibreglass columns or mass-produced rotundas will rarely fit a particular site, even if they are well designed in themselves – which is not always the case. However, building a small, well-proportioned, classical portico is not so difficult if a little investigation of architectural orders is first carried out. Vitruvius's textbooks and Banister Fletcher's *A History of Architecture* (IXXX) give a clear account of the optical corrections employed in classical architecture, as well as formulae for calculating proportions and the entasis for a column.

The entasis is an essential refinement for columns where the shaft begins to diminish in thickness, almost imperceptibly, from about a third of the way up from the base. Its purpose is to counteract the hollow appearance which would be given by straight-sided columns. It is also important to give the major horizontals a slightly convex shape: even for a small garden temple this should apply to the steps and the entablature above the columns. Temples should be raised on at least three steps. Vitruvius recommended that the number of steps should always be an odd number in order to start the ascent and arrive at the temple on your right foot.

Although they can resemble a garden temple, pavilions have a more utilitarian function, either for occasional entertainment or for residential use. In France, especially during the eighteenth century, the pavilion was a miniature palace built, for example, to house a royal mistress.

Being small, they had none of the pretensions of the palace, but all the charm of a building designed to decorate the garden or park. The rococo style of design was often used for the interior decoration.

Chinese Garden Buildings

Europeans began receiving accounts of Chinese gardens from travellers during the second half of the seventeenth century. William Temple, in his *Upon the Gardens of Epicurus, or, of Gardening, in the Year 1685* (1692), wrote that the Chinese scorned the formal concept of garden design and that 'their greatest Reach of Imagination is employed in contriving Figures, where the Beauty shall be great, and strike the Eye, but without any Order or Disposition of Parts, that shall be commonly or easily observ'd'. Patterns on imported porcelain, lacquerwork and silks gave Europeans glimpses of these gardens laid out 'without Order or Disposition to Parks', in which there was at least one garden building. An Italian priest, Father Ripa, completed a series of views of the Imperial palace and its gardens at Jehol in Manchuria in 1713, and these were published in album-form on his return to Europe eleven years later. At least one copy was purchased by Lord Burlington, William Kent's patron. Working at the same time as Kent were a number of talented garden owners who experimented with the new landscape style of gardening; some used Chinese garden buildings as decorative features. These early light-hearted essays in landscape gardening, with their Chinese-style buildings, are now referred to as rococo and they had a parallel in interior decoration. Because of a lack of detailed information, these chinoiserie garden buildings were not truly authentic, although very appealing to European eyes.

Chinoiserie buildings were of three main types: the kiosk, the simplest, had open sides and provided seating within; the house, based on an enclosed study or studio; and the multi-storey structure, called a pagoda, designed to be viewed from any direction. They were mostly constructed in timber, which was colourfully painted – often with red lacquer and sometimes with cream lattice panels and gilt decoration. The up-turning roof lines had dragon motifs carved into them and bells suspended from the roof-end projections.

To the Chinese, a garden had not been completed until it had a traditional garden building, whose strong colouring made up for the lack of plant interest in the winter scene. Although they possessed the richest

The Chinese pavilion is reflected in the pool at Hill Court, Herefordshire.

A Chinese Garden

The Chinese style of garden design, 'Sharawadji', is associated with the naturalistic movement of the early eighteenth-century. It was a style that called for the use of buildings in the landscape, but this fundamental was apparently misunderstood in Europe and particularly in England, where garden buildings tended to be over-powering features standing in splendid isolation, like the pagoda at Kew Gardens, near London. The Chinese, in contrast, used garden buildings within relatively confined areas to combine practicality and aesthetics.

Few people today can indulge in building without specific need, but a building undeniably adds charm to a garden. A garage, garden shed or extra room can be conceived as a garden building instead of a conventional home extension, and linked to the main house by a covered walkway. Instead of losing half the garden, you would make two, smaller gardens. The pleasure of a garden, after all, is not determined by its size – a concept that has been an integral part of Chinese landscape planning

for thousands of years. A building could convey a Chinese style by using simple Chinese lattice patterns made of timber and painted lacquer red.

It is ironic that the so-called Chinese style of gardening was popular in Europe a century before the majority of Chinese plants became available. With such a beautiful native flora it is not surprising that the Chinese favoured a natural style of gardening, in which rock work was often featured. Below is a selection of plants that would be appropriate for a Chinese garden.

Anemone hupehensis, Parthenocissus henryana, Paeonia lactiflora, P. suffruticosa, Viburnum fragrans, Chaenomeles speciosa, Clematis tangutica, C. armandii, Ginko biloba, Prunus dulcis (Almond), Hemerocallis (Day lilies), Salix matsudana 'Pendula', Iris (Sibiricae group), Juniperus chinensis 'Pfitzeriana', Lilium tigrinum, L. regale, Magnolia liliiflora, Jasminum nudiflorum, Arundinaria nitida (bamboo), Wisteria sinensis, Cornus alba

store of temperate garden plants, the Chinese restricted the plants in their gardens to those traditionally associated with moral qualities or having emotional status.

Very few garden buildings in the chinoiserie style have survived; any re-creations must be designed from pattern-books such as William and John Halfpenny's *New Designs for Chinese Temples* (1750); William Chambers's *Designs of Chinese Buildings* (1757); Charles Over's *Ornamental Architecture in the Gothic, Chinese and Modern Taste* (1758); Le Rouge's *Detail des Nouveaux Jardins à la Mode* (1776-1787); and from the paintings of Thomas Robins, many of which have been reproduced in *Gardens of Delight, The Rococo English Landscape of Thomas Robins* (1977) by John Harris.

By the 1760s in Britain, the rococo garden with its Chinese buildings had been superseded by the landscape park, where more substantial garden buildings in stone were required. But in Europe, until the end of the century, the landscape park was frequently ornamented with at least one Chinese building. During the early years of the next century, when specialized gardens were once again being sited near the house, some Chinese buildings were constructed as centre-pieces and pagodas acted as viewing towers. By the Victorian age, oriental garden buildings were more likely to be Japanese in style, copied or originating from the numerous international exhibitions held during this period. Sometimes they were simply used as a summerhouse in the flower garden, but,

increasingly, towards the end of the century, they were an integral part of a re-created Japanese-style garden.

Gothick Garden Buildings

Proponents of the eighteenth-century revived Gothick style used clanking armour, baronial wars, skeletal hermits and masonry walls that would give a 'deep and hollow groan' to evoke the medieval world – and nowhere was this more manifest than in garden making.

Sanderson Miller, the English amateur architect and landscape gardener and the connoisseur and writer Horace Walpole, were two important figures in promoting this, the alternative to the classical and chinoiserie styles. Miller became renowned for his designs for ruined mock castles and arches. The dovecote built as a Gothick tower in 1745 at Wroxton Abbey, Oxfordshire, and the mock castle at Hagley Hall in the West Midlands, built three years later, are good examples of Miller's work.

There was no equivalent of classical temples in medieval times, and consequently the designs for Gothick garden buildings were evolved from medieval fortress towers or abbey ruins. Towers, hermits' houses, archways, mock castles and ruins were built, as well as distant eye-catchers, such as faked picturesque battlements to an estate farmhouse. The Gothick created by these eighteenth century enthusiasts was, of course, only superficially following authentic Gothic style; to distinguish it from the genuine, it is given a 'k' in its spelling.

Medieval Gothic crosses, crocketed pinnacles and arches rescued from demolished buildings also decorated the landscape garden. Occasionally, today, Gothic ornaments can be found to decorate a landscape garden; Victorian architecture

Gothick summerhouse or alcove built in local stone about 1770 at Barnsley House, Gloucestershire.

abounded with Gothic-style ornamentation, which can form a key piece in the reconstruction of a Gothic-flavoured garden summerhouse or be used simply as an ornament.

Follies, Ruins, Grottoes and Hermits' Houses

Follies and Ruins

The different emotions that could be evoked during a walk in the landscape garden added greatly to the aesthetic experience. Landscape theorists and practitioners explored the responses that could be enjoyed from the beautiful, sublime feelings of melancholy, nostalgia and the importance of association. The sublime in the landscape garden represented an experience that contained an element of terror or chill to the senses, as might be

Tufa lined walls and pebble-patterned floor in the Grotto at Stourhead, circa 1748. The nymph is of painted lead.

gained from viewing and contemplating a dimly lit grotto, a hermit's cell, or the ruins of some ancient structure. Sometimes the site for a landscape garden contained medieval ruins, and these would be readily incorporated into the design. Where they did not exist, it was not uncommon to introduce artificial ruins, such as small castles, arches and monastic buildings. Similar folly-like buildings were sham in that they were designed to deceive the viewer, especially from a distance: look-out towers on hills outside the garden might be only one-sided, and farmhouses would be given battlements and other medieval features in order to catch the eye and give a sense of nostalgia to the scene.

Follies, in fact, came in all shapes and forms; now any unusual and eccentric building in the landscape or garden has come to be classified as one. The height of folly-building coincided with the landscape garden, but they are still erected today. There are no pattern-books or rules for them: they are essentially very personal expressions, unconsciously but markedly eccentric, and arise from the owner's desire to build in a non-architectural and non-utilitarian way.

Grottoes

The grotto goes back at least to the gardens of the Italian Renaissance, where it was usually given an entrance front that had some architectural elements in it.

The grotto for the landscape garden was more natural looking, something discovered by accident, although the entrance was emphasized. Built into hillsides, under lakes, on islands in lakes, and into artificial mounds, grottoes were constructed like an understorey of a building and covered with soil, rocks and vegetation. Inside, a passage would lead to one or more chambers that could be used for social gatherings; some included an invigorating cold bath. Side passages might display appropriate statues, dramatically lit by shafts of light coming from an opening in the roof. Their interior decoration gave much entertainment to the owners, who collected shells, stalactites, glistening or translucent minerals, and even bones and fossils, for lining the walls and roof. If the grotto was sited close to water, views were provided through openings and interesting light reflections were created in the inside of the grotto. Running spring water flowing through the grotto was a favourite touch, giving scope for cold baths, statues of water gods and nymphs.

Grottoes in conservatories were usually much more modest affairs; sometimes little more than a rocky cavern, made from well-arranged rockwork and with sufficient light to grow ferns, mosses and selaginellas. Rock that has an interesting and weathered surface, such as tufa, was always favoured for the rockwork in the interior of a grotto at this time.

Hermits' Houses

Hermits' houses were sometimes built in the more remote parts of a landscape garden. They were usually asymmetrical in design, presumably to add to their eccentricity. To see smoke rising from the hermit's chimney on a winter's day domesticated the wilderness aspect of the landscape. Houses that have survived were built in stone, as at Stowe, Buckinghamshire, but many others were constructed in

timber. The 'hermit' was in fact recruited from advertisements in local newspapers. In return for remuneration he had to live according to a set of rules. Most contemporary accounts suggest that the successful applicant did not stay with the post for very long.

Bridges

Any stream or river in the Renaissance and the landscape garden would have been looked upon as an opportunity to construct a grand architectural feature: it might contain a suite of rooms at either side or, as in the Palladian model, a covered superstructure similar to a colonnade. The bridge was constructed in stone and given a well-proportioned segmental arch spring-

Chinese-style painted timber bridge supported by piers at Pusey House, Berks.

ing from close to the water level, and the fine side elevation was made doubly pleasing when reflected in clear water.

With the increased number of exotic plants available during the nineteenth century, there was more emphasis on the wealth of plant forms and foliage in the garden composition. Since then garden bridges have usually been more modest structures, predominantly of timber construction. However, the best-designed bridges are still elegant, with some influences from Chinese and Japanese gardens being apparent in arched beam constructions, details of balustrading, provision for seats on a platform section, and an overhead superstructure for the support of such flowering climbing plants as wisteria.

Sham bridges were built in the eighteenth-century landscape garden as decoration, but also to deceive the eye into believing that there was one large lake, rather than a series of small ponds. The mock bridge at Kenwood House, London, in painted timber to resemble stonework is a good surviving example of this landscape *trompe l'oeil*.

A garden bridge should be seen in side elevation with its reflection, and the layout of the garden and its paths must make the most of this. The best preparation for deciding on the design of a timber footbridge is to take some measured sketch notes of construction and proportions from good existing examples.

Ice-Houses

Most important houses in the eighteenth century possessed an ice-house sited in a cool and well-drained part of the gardens. They were capable of storing winter ice for up to two years, for the making of ice-cream, filling wine coolers and for the treatment of sprains. Ice-houses were usually sunken egg-shaped stone or brick buildings, with a drainage pit at the bottom, lined outside with clay, and covered with soil. The entrance was down steps to a passageway which had several doors. They were not ornamental features of a garden, although occasionally decorative additions above ground were added.

Tree Houses

Small timber houses built in the more horizontal angled branches of a large tree, in order to afford a better view or an exciting playhouse for children, have been constructed in gardens at least since the mid-eighteenth century. Sometimes the building was intended to be permanent and built in an architectural style of the period. Probably the oldest surviving example is at Pitchford Hall, Shropshire, which has glazed windows and decorative interior plasterwork. It is built in a lime (Linden) tree, a fairly long-lived tree, and so has remained intact. Recent restoration has been carried out to this tree-house, and the large horizontally growing branches have been supported with cables.

Tree-houses were popular retreats in a number of late nineteenth-century gardens; the design was often given some novel feature such as a round window-opening. Stepped ladders are usually provided for permanent access to the tree-house.

Root-Houses, Rustic Houses and Moss-Houses
Root-Houses and Rustic Houses
A special form of rustic work, which originated in the landscape garden but was most popular in the flower garden, employed large tree roots, although more often the stool or base of the tree, to form or

This rustic summerhouse designed by Shirley Hibberd appeared in 'The National Magazine', 1857.

portions of unbarked timber'. For the preparation and treatment of the rustic apple branches, Hibberd advised that 'they should be sawed up into proper lengths, and then steeped in boiling water to loosen the bark; then well dried, worked into their places, and varnished'. To varnish rustic woodwork he recommended the following procedure: 'Wash the woodwork with soap and water; and when dry, wash it again with boiled linseed oil, choosing a hot sunny day for the operation. A few days after, varnish it twice with hard varnish, and it will last for years.'

Never should rustic summerhouses 'be placed in clean open spots of grass and flowers', Hibberd adds. 'Better to site them on a mound surrounded by shrubs and trees, rootwork, rockeries, ferneries and water scenery.' This, of course, was written before croquet and lawn tennis became popular, when summerhouses were needed to store equipment and as shady pavilions close to the place of play.

At the turn of the century timber summerhouses in the Swiss style were popular, with patterns of fir cones forming the interior decoration.

Moss-Houses

Moss-houses had timber frames, which were covered by latticework, with moss and lichen in between the laths and held in place by wire or cord. 'The great art', wrote Mrs Loudon in *The Ladies' Companion to the Flower Garden*, 'consists in arranging the moss so as to form a pattern: and this is accomplished by sorting the moss into heaps of the different colours, tracing the patterns rudely on the laths, and keeping a coloured copy.' The roof was normally thatched, but sometimes it was covered with moss-covered bark from old oak or pine trees.

be the basis of a small garden house. Sections of the stool with its roots were used to make the walls and the root-house acted as a covered seat sited to embrace an interesting view or, in the second half of the nineteenth century, was placed close to the lawn used for croquet and lawn tennis. William Shenstone, a pioneer landscape theorist and practitioner, had a root-house in his landscape garden at the Leasowes, near Birmingham.

Shirley Hibberd, in the *National Magazine* of 1857, gives a description of this contemporary practice. He recommends that the structural members be of unbarked oak, with selected toppings of old apple wood used for the lattice work. The apple branches should be varnished 'so as to stand out brightly amongst the darker

Thatched summerhouse at Broadwell House of a type popular in late Victorian and Edwardian flower gardens.

This post Second World War summerhouse can be revolved to face the sun.

Summerhouses

The most common garden building since the eighteenth century is the summerhouse. Many nineteenth-century examples were built in rusticwork and given a thatched roof. The more substantial summerhouses had walls made up of masonry up to the window height, which were covered in decorative patterns of rustic branches. The summerhouse had windows and a door, and was used as a pavilion for lawn games, for tea, as a quiet room for study and as a garden house for the children.

During the first part of the twentieth century and until the Second World War, more architectural styles were used for the design of summerhouses, especially if an architect had been employed on the garden layout. The design invariably reflected the style of the house. Numerous examples are illustrated in garden books of the period, notably in *Gardens for Small Country Houses* by Jekyll and Weaver, first published in 1910, but reprinted in 1981.

During the 1930s the fashion for suntans led to summerhouses having large windows facing south, and sometimes the whole structure could be rotated to follow the sun.

13
CREATING
THE MOOD

How successfully the recreation of a garden that has its roots in history has been achieved, how distinctive the mood that it conveys, depends on the sureness of touch with which it has been styled, upon the standards by which it is maintained, and by the light in which it is seen most often.

All gardens exist more vividly in the mind than on the ground. They remain at their best in the imagination, since nature can never be totally commanded. 'You should have been here last week' is much more than a stage joke. Its implications are inevitable: no garden is the same two weeks running, or even for two days – it is in a constant condition of change. Translated on to the ground, the imagination's vision can always be seen to be capable of improvement. The most skilled and inventive of garden designers work not only from plans: they insist on putting in the pegs themselves and placing the plants with their own hands. This involves endless walking to and fro, considering everything from every possible angle, and much digging and repositioning until the eye is at last satisfied. The ultimate aim is to capture a mood and make it possible for this to be summoned at will.

Most often this will be recaptured at one time of day. All gardens are seen at their most captivating in the evening, when the sun has sunk, the breeze has dropped, and before the dusk has gathered so thickly as to merge all in approaching night. Just before then, though, a garden works its most potent magic. All imperfections are dissolved and all the elements are brought into their closest relationship. Lines are softened. Vistas really do enshrine the distance. Recesses, embrasures and enclosures become invested with mystery. Garden houses, gazebos, even utilitarian greenhouses and toolsheds, seem to hold some strange but benign spirits. Statues seem ready to step from their plinths like the outraged Commendatore in *Don Giovanni*. The strongest element is the mood.

Anyone setting out to make a period garden should take care to compose the scene from the windows of the house; it is

Plants encroaching over the path give an impression of sweet disorder, enhanced by the gnarled old apple tree. Too much garden management will kill a garden's spirit.

from here that it can be enjoyed in all weathers. Hence the importance not only of composing the picture so that the proportions of its elements are good, but that they stand in the right relationship to one another; that perspective is set up to give an illusion of space and distance, and that the fusion of styles is well judged.

Combining the Elements

Many historic buildings belong to different periods, showing the progression of tastes and techniques. In the same way, period gardens are likely to draw from several ages and geographical influences. The former Tudor palace of Hampton Court, although illustrating the whole history of garden design over several centuries and embellished with modern plantings, nevertheless presents itself as a unity. Because its different styles were carefully matched, the progression from one to the

other is measured: the whole seems to have been composed by one presiding genius with a sure touch.

To secure the mood of a period garden, disparate elements of style must be kept securely apart. If you were creating an Elizabethan knot you would not plant it with showy modern petunias but with flowers that, if not exactly contemporary, would have some historical affinity with the box or lavender patterning. The great eighteenth-century garden of Stourhead, in Wiltshire, England, is heavily decorated with modern rhododendrons which mar the serenity of the carefully contrived landscape, originally composed of trees, water, expanses of turf and classical and romantic buildings. And evergreen hebes of New Zealand origin were planted in a celebrated early twentieth-century garden; they were out of character and did not merge, and were therefore discordant.

Sometimes several elements that derive from different times and places can be combined successfully, the mood preserved by unifying the scene with living as well as inanimate materials. Hedges are the easiest way to achieve this, and next comes stone, either natural or reconstituted.

Rather than create a period garden that calls for, perhaps, walls of rough-hewn stone in a district where there is no natural stone, it would be better to choose a scheme in which paths and walls were made largely of brick or dressed stone. But the same element should not be used throughout. The Spanish garden at Mount Stewart near Belfast, in Northern Ireland, merges with the whole – despite the bright green Andalusian tiles of its loggia – because its pool and its steps are made of the same local stone as the rest of the architectural features of the whole garden. There is a change of mood in this section but not a discordant one.

In essence, then, the period garden being recreated should not be widely at variance with the local traditions and materials; or if it is, the garden should be made to merge by using some materials that do have an affinity to both style and locality, or by grafting on some element common to both – a link with the house, either in stone or style, or a unifying element of similar vegetation, for example.

A Sense of Timelessness

The closely shorn lawn is a modern concept. Once turf was cut by scythe, expertly but never so closely as a machine cut. Weedkillers had not been invented. Where there is turf in a garden built in an old style, the blades of the machine used on it should be kept high, and if daisies, plantains and selfheal weeds invade the grass it

will only aid the sense of timelessness. They need only be reduced or removed when they threaten to take over.

Nor should herbaceous plants be lifted and divided. If they are allowed to grow into big clumps they may not flower as profusely, but nevertheless will contribute more to the atmosphere. If they want to loll let them, rather than offering canes as supports, although old-fashioned flowers usually maintain a comfortable stockiness. Similarly, those that want to creep should

The carved figure adorning the shrouded garden shed adds an air of mystery to this corner of Iford Manor garden in Wiltshire, particularly at dusk.

Brightly-coloured moss can be encouraged to grow between the bricks of a herringbone path, disguising unattractive mortar.

Galvanized iron watering cans blend inoffensively with the garden in a way that plastic ones never do.

be allowed to flow on to paths and between taller plants, and especially over masonry.

Giving new brickwork and stonework the appearance of age is not so difficult as it may seem: there are short cuts to achieving the appearance that time slowly puts upon them. When bricks are laid, the joints should be rubbed with a blunt-ended stick rather than pointed carefully with a trowel. Whenever possible, 'second-hand' bricks reclaimed from old buildings should be used.

After paving has been laid it is best grouted by brushing over it a dry cement mortar mix, which falls into the cracks and solidifies with the help of the natural moisture in the atmosphere. Moss will soon grow on this, and outline each slab.

Nothing puts the patina of age on a garden more certainly than lichens, those very primitive forms of life that always

appear on anything left lying out of doors exposed to the elements. In a recreated garden they are to be encouraged by a simple stratagem: lichen will grow very quickly on brick or stonework that has been painted with cow dung mixed in a bucket of water – the sovereign method of subduing new-looking masonry. At first the brick, stone or concrete will discolour, at once adding years to its appearance, then a haze of green will appear, soon to give way to a welcome encrustation. Once it has taken hold the lichen itself will offer fertile ground for the spores of ferns to settle or for the odd inoffensive weed. However, it is better to grow plants of your own choosing on walls and in pockets in masonry such as the houseleeks that can subsist on nothing but detritus, or wall-flowers that will send roots deep into loosening mortar in search of the little moisture they need.

Hardwood timber furniture soon takes on its own patina under the effect of weathering – especially if one resists the temptation to treat it against decay with preservative, which prevents algae grow-ing. Hardwoods, in fact, have a very long life without this agency.

For added comfort, as well as for aesthe-tic reasons, it is always wise to give garden seats a setting of an exedra-like hedge behind them for protection from the wind; this also makes the seats seem important decorative objects.

Although a seat should be placed in such a position that it will command a view of a vista, it often gives a vacant, unoccupied air to the scene when it is used as the focal point. Instead, this is the place for an ornament, a figure, a pillar, an urn or a vase to give significance to the prospect; but the important thing is that it should be large enough to make its point with emphasis.

A whole garden could be built around this mysterious pair, standing at Charlton Mackrell Court, Somerset. Choose statuary carefully as it casts a powerful aura.

An old garden roller is both useful and conducive to creating a period mood.

Ivy and roses are both evocative plants, to be used with discretion. Here they shroud the fountain walk at Villa Noailles in Italy with an aura of timelessness, while also shading the path and covering unsightly posts.

Disguise and Sweet Disorder

Nothing can be done quickly to give plastic urns and ornaments the patina of age, except to discolour them by painting with mud, although this is easily washed off by rain. But some will remain if the crevices are sufficiently deep, allowing algae to form on the fragments of soil left. The best method of disguise is to grow fairly rampant evergreen trailing plants in them. Here the variegated-leaved periwinkles are specially useful and can be attractive. If

(above) The glass veranda outside this Edwardian house was too narrow to be useful. In order to provide a worthwhile extension, beams supported on reconstituted stone columns had sheets of corrugated perspex fitted between them on a slight fall, to throw off the rain. Vines trained out on wire beneath the roof made a leafy ceiling, and the resulting open-sided room was furnished in summer with Victorian iron furniture and straw mats, lit by wall lights and warmed by radiant heaters fitted over the glazed doors to the drawing room. On the steps a large collection of containers, ranging from egg crocks to an old washing copper, were filled with bedding plants for seasonal colour.

(left) Self-seeded plants growing in walls will create just the right mood of natural disorder.

(above right) The Sweet Bay pavilion at Villa Noailles is the focal point of this charming little area.

(right) This comfortable sunfilled conservatory belonged to that master of 'creating the mood', Cecil Beaton.

plastic hoses have to be left about the garden, then black ones are better; they resemble the outdated rubber type.

Where standpipes for garden watering are set up, build them into a little brick pillar and cement to this one of the ceramic wall basins which are pierced for a tap and are imported from Italy and Spain, where they are made on traditional models. They do have to be wrapped up in winter, though, to prevent frost spoiling the glaze.

Plastic can be acceptable in the period garden on some occasions, however. The same pillars that are used today for modern houses built in the Georgian style can be employed in gardens in the construction of pergolas and arbours. A cheaper method of building such features would be to set up concrete pillars in the ground and sheath them with tan-coloured plastic netting and allow climbing plants to entwine them. Again, plastic could be used as concealed roofing for a concrete post or timber-built arbour using the transparent sheeting.

The sweet disorder that suggests age and contributes so potently to the mood of a period garden is created most readily by climbing plants swagging walls and fences, sheds and other outbuildings, pergolas, arbours and bowers. Provided it is not allowed its head, even ivy can be used in the small-leaved variegated forms sold as house plants. Managing climbing plants so that they are made to look as though they are part of time's magic, and not of its all-engulfing destructive work, calls for constant pinching and directing, however, as well as the use of the secateurs as though they were a sculptor's chisel or a painter's brush. It is in exercising such skills and judgements that the worlds of gardener and artist merge.

INDEX